A VIEW OF BERG'S *LULU*
THROUGH THE AUTOGRAPH SOURCES

A VIEW OF BERG'S *LULU* THROUGH THE AUTOGRAPH SOURCES

Patricia Hall

University of California Press
Berkeley Los Angeles London

University of California Press
Berkeley and Los Angeles, California

University of California Press, Ltd.
London, England

© 1996 by
The Regents of the University of California

Library of Congress Cataloging-in-Publication Data
Hall, Patricia
　　A view of Berg's "Lulu" through the autograph sources / Patricia
Hall.
　　　　p.　cm.
　　Includes bibliographical references and index.
　　ISBN 0-520-08819-0
　　1. Berg, Alban, 1885–1935. Lulu.　2. Operas—Analysis,
appreciation.　I. Title.
ML410.B47H35　1996
782.1—dc20　　　　　　　　　　　　　　　　　　　　　95-40543
　　　　　　　　　　　　　　　　　　　　　　　　　　　　　CIP
　　　　　　　　　　　　　　　　　　　　　　　　　　　　　MN

9 8 7 6 5 4 3 2 1

To my parents

Contents

Acknowledgments   ix

Introduction   2

I. Berg's Sketches: Format and Compositional Process   15

II. Chronology of the Autograph Sources   28

III. The Interaction of Role and Form   61

IV. Derivational Unfoldings: The Case of Dr. Schön   89

V. The Progress of a Method: Berg's Tone Rows for *Lulu*   109

VI. Why Is Berg's Twelve-Tone Music So Difficult to Analyze?   128

Concluding Remarks   161

Notes   164

Works Cited   175

Index   179

Acknowledgments

I have labored nearly as long on this book as Berg did on his opera. Unlike Berg, however, I seem to have survived to complete the project.

At UC Press, Stephanie Fay carefully edited my manuscript, kept the project moving, and has been a pleasure to work with the whole time. Steve Renick patiently answered innumerable questions about layout. And Doris Kretschmer had enough faith in this project to see it through to the end.

A Fulbright Fellowship allowed me to complete the initial research for this project. Since that time UCSB has generously supported my work with Faculty Research Grants and Faculty Career Development Awards.

Pieter van den Toorn, David Lewin, Reinhardt Strohm, Allen Forte, and Robert Morgan read parts of the manuscript and made many invaluable suggestions. Pieter's unerring logic, in particular, helped me sort out the circuitous path of the Introduction. Michael Beckerman was a truly supportive colleague and gave me the right advice when I needed it most.

Julianne Brand, Christopher Hailey, Reinhard Strohm, and Rosemary Hilmar took the time to scrutinize Berg's many illegible annotations. Janet Naudé has a remarkable talent for detecting inaccuracies; I thank her for being a supportive friend during this whole endeavor, and for proofreading the entire manuscript.

Greg Betz, who is now beginning his photographic career in New York City, produced the computer images of the original sketches. William Koseluk, a superb pianist as well as Manager of the Microcomputer Lab at UCSB, always discovered a way to accomplish a task even when it supposedly "couldn't be done." I thank him for magically converting Commodore files to Macintosh, for putting in many long hours gratis on the examples, and for devising methods to computerize my often extremely difficult transcriptions.

A special thanks to Dr. Joseph Gmeiner of the Music Division of the Austrian National Library for making my research in Vienna such a pleasant experience. Dr. Ernst Hilmar of the Wiener Stadt- und Landesbibliothek allowed me to read transcriptions of certain letters, and suggested correspondence that was critical to read.

Over the years Martha Hyde has been my advisor, mentor, and friend. She is also the only scholar I am aware of who has used twelve-tone sketches analytically. I cannot begin to thank her enough for her dedication to this project; as a professor myself now, I appreciate her even more.

Above all, I should thank my parents, who cared enough to learn about the peculiar world of academia. Without them I am not sure I could have met the challenge of Yale and single parenthood, and it is to them this book is dedicated.

Parts of the Introduction, Chapters 1, 2, and 6, and the Conclusion were originally published in *The Berg Companion,* ed. Douglas Jarman (London: Macmillan, 1989), pp. 235–259. Reproduced by permission of Macmillan Press Ltd. Chapter 3 was originally published in *Alban Berg: Historical and Analytical Perspectives,* ed. David Gable and Robert Morgan (Oxford: Oxford University Press, 1991), pp. 235–259. Reproduced by permission of Oxford University Press. Chapter 5 was originally published in the *Musical Quarterly* 71 (1985): 500–519. Reproduced by permission of Oxford University Press, New York.

Examples 1, 2, 3a, and 3b are reproduced by permission of the *Journal of Music Theory* (© Yale University).

Excerpts of Berg's letters to Joseph Polnauer, Leo Schiedrowitz, Rudolph Kolisch, and Anton Webern are reproduced with the permission of the Wiener Stadtbibliothek. All quotations from Berg's published works are reproduced by permission of Universal Edition, A.G., Vienna. Berg's sketches are reproduced from the original sources by permission of the Alban Berg Stiftung and the Music Division of the Austrian National Library, Vienna.

All translations are my own unless otherwise noted.

Introduction

Die Oper *Lulu* gehört zu den Werken, die ihre ganze Qualität desto mehr erweisen, je länger und tiefer man in sie sich versenkt.[1]

The opera *Lulu* is one of those works that reveal their full quality the longer and deeper one immerses oneself in them.

Theodor Adorno

After fifty years of analysis and commentary we are only beginning to understand the quality and complexity of Berg's most important twelve-tone work. Our initial insights into the opera—those conveyed by Berg to his student Willi Reich—appeared as program notes for the first performance of the *Lulu Suite* in November 1934 and as a longer article published almost a year after Berg's death in December 1935.[2] The article briefly described the opera's essential structural components: the tone rows, the methods of row derivation, the overall form, the dramatic intent. Though it was introductory, its degree of detail held the promise of accuracy and interpretive insight, especially since it apparently conveyed the unadulterated ideas of the composer himself. As Reich notes in the introduction to his biography of Berg, in which he repeats much of this material: "Even in the section devoted to his work I have only used texts that were written by the composer himself, or at least under his supervision and with his consent. Happily such texts cover all his major works, and complete authenticity can be claimed for this section as well."[3] Unhappily, as we have now come to realize, this authenticity was frequently laden with vagaries and imprecision, for Berg was in fact reluctant to describe the details of his compositional method even to his closest students—much less to his reading public.

Inaccuracies in Berg's statements were initially discussed by George Perle, whose research on *Lulu* represents the first substantive theoretical study of the work. Perle's article "The Music of *Lulu:* A New Analysis" challenges as well as augments Berg's analysis.[4] I discuss these findings in some detail in Chapter 4, but for now what is relevant is Perle's primary goal: to establish how Berg's use of the twelve-tone system differs significantly from Schoenberg's. The differences include Berg's derivation of subsidiary rows from the source row, the use of unordered rows, and the use of "a pervasive harmonic atmosphere based on the preferential use of certain sonorities" that serve to associate specific row forms.[5] Perle goes on to argue that Berg's statements, less analytical in intent than Reich's phrase "authorized analysis" suggests, are a defense of those twelve-tone procedures that depart from or contradict those of Schoenberg:

> The authorized analysis of *Lulu* is not concerned with the music of *Lulu*, but only with presenting evidence that Berg's use of more than one set is not in violation of one of Schoenberg's principal tenets of twelve-tone composition ("It does not seem right to me to use more than one series.") . . . *Lulu,* although profoundly indebted to Schoenberg's technical discoveries, is not based on the principles of his twelve-tone system.[6]

Perle's articles as well as his subsequent book on *Lulu* represent the most detailed and perceptive analytical study of the opera available.[7] In addition to defining Berg's idiosyncratic style of row association, both Perle and Douglas Jarman have investigated Berg's pitch and rhythmic organization and its interpretative relation to the drama.

In 1959 Berg's widow, Helene Berg, deposited the first of Berg's autograph manuscripts in the Musiksammlung of the Österreichische Nationalbibliothek.[8] The complete collection of autograph manuscripts for *Lulu* became accessible to scholars in 1981, beginning a new and promising phase in *Lulu* scholarship. Again, Reich, Perle, and Jarman have made important contributions to this new area of research. As with his analyses, Reich received sketches for *Lulu* directly from Berg and often cited them in later articles to counter Perle's objections—or rather, what he perceived as Perle's objections.[9] Perle's use of the autograph sources, in contrast, might be termed restorative. During a brief examination of the *Particell* in the summer of 1963, Perle discovered a detailed outline of the scenario for the Film Music that superseded the sketch previously published by Reich; he also supplied the role doublings for the third act based on "otherwise inexplicable musical correspondences."[10] (These doublings and triplings were later verified by a sketch discovered by Douglas Jarman.)[11] In addition, during his brief study of the autograph sources in 1981, Perle discovered Berg's working typescript of his libretto, which contained the text for the missing quartet of Act III, scene 2.[12]

Jarman's study of the sketches was somewhat abbreviated since, like Perle's, it predated the official accessibility of the autograph sources. His article "*Lulu:* The Sketches" summarizes his observations and emphasizes those sketches that deal with row derivation, rhythmic organization, and multiple roles.[13] In *The Music of Alban Berg* he repeats many of these observations, as well as including information from the sketches for other works.[14] Although chronology and compositional process—the traditional realm of sketch study—occasionally enter into his work, as a theorist Jarman is primarily concerned with the analytical potential of the sketches, that is, what they reveal about the music or what analytical problems they resolve that might otherwise be misinterpreted or overlooked. I continue in this tradition in the present work. This book represents the first detailed analytical study of the sketches for *Lulu,* as well as other related autograph material and previously inaccessible correspondence to Berg in the Österreichische Nationalbibliothek. Although the existing analytical work on *Lulu* has been vital for understanding the opera, my thesis is that many of its theoretical and analytical issues can best be resolved through study of the autograph sources.

The usefulness of sketches for analysis has been a much debated topic among Beethoven scholars. Douglas Johnson, the instigator of this debate, argues that the sketches show us nothing that is not already apparent from the finished score.[15] While Johnson's statement might suggest that characteristics inherent in Beethoven's sketches make them difficult to use for analysis, it is also likely that many of these difficulties arise from the compositional system the sketches draw upon. In the discussion that follows I briefly examine two of these systems, tonality and extended tonality, to identify some of the challenges that they pose for sketch study. With this information, we can more readily understand the properties of Berg's sketches that make them valuable for analysis.

Tonality within the common practice period is a highly defined and comprehensible compositional system. At its most rudimentary level, it is possible to categorize every note of a passage in terms of a particular harmony, or nonharmony. Moreover, the harmonies themselves have specific functions and syntax: a II_6 chord usually acts as a pre-dominant; a V_3^4 chord often passes between a I and I_6. But this comprehensibility also limits our use of sketches; the system is so well understood that—as Johnson argues—there is little we cannot discover about a passage simply by looking at the music.

This clarity of system extends to more subtle levels of analysis as well. In his article on the sketches for Beethoven's Sonata Opus 14, no. 1, Schachter focuses almost entirely on the unifying properties of a single motivic figure: the ascending fourth, B, C sharp, D sharp, E.[16] Schachter finds only two instances in which the extant sketches provide analytical insight. In the first, evidence of Beethoven's compositional intent (shown in sketches for the exposition) clarifies a revision in the recapitulation. This evidence sensitizes us to an analytic detail in the first theme of the recapitulation that would probably otherwise go unnoticed. Specifically, Schachter cites Beethoven's repeated but unsuccessful attempts to retain the ascending fourth motive at its original transposition level in the bridge section and second theme. The sketches lead Schachter to question whether Beethoven transposed the left-hand run appearing in the bridge (Example 1) and moved it to the first theme to retain the B, E ascending fourth that ends the figure (Example 2).

EXAMPLE 1. Sketch of bridge of recapitulation

EXAMPLE 2. Final version: beginning of recapitulation

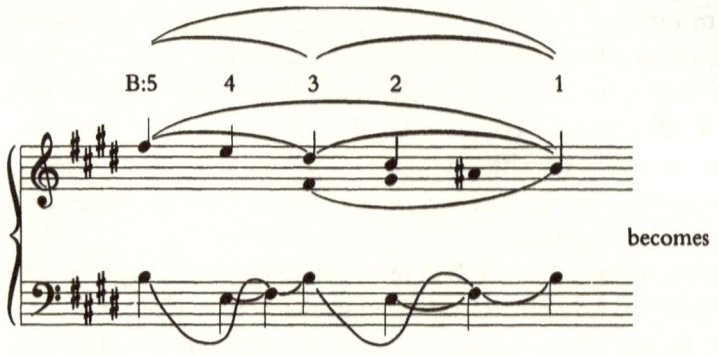

EXAMPLE 3A. Voice leading graph of second theme of exposition (sketch)

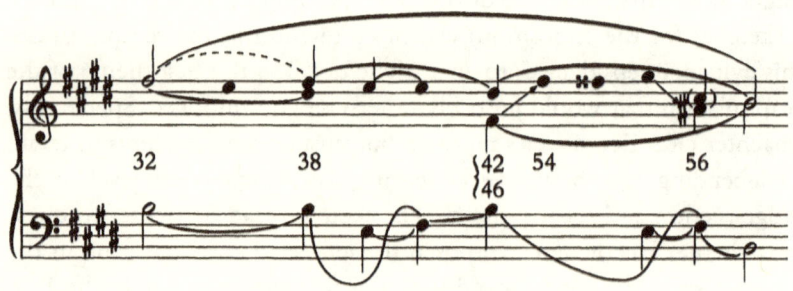

EXAMPLE 3B. Voice leading graph of second theme of exposition (final version)

In Schachter's second instance, a more subtle, but also potentially more problematic, use of sketches has parallels with Berg's own compositional process: a musical idea, presented in an unequivocal form in the sketches, is elaborated into a more remote form in the final version. Schachter cites a sketch of the second theme of the exposition that shows a descent from scale degree 5 to 1 in the upper voice (Example 3a). In the final version, however, a register transfer of an inner voice "suppresses" the C sharp and moves to scale degree 1, and the C sharp is merely implied (Example 3b). In this instance, Beethoven has revised his sketch, but rather than being a "failed experiment," the sketch elucidates the underlying structure of this motive in the final version.

Schachter focuses on sketches that suggest analytical insights, but he also stresses those that confirm analytical ideas derived through study of the finished score:

> Finding confirmation for one's ideas is a large and highly important part of the analytical process and ought not to be dismissed as of negligible value. Besides, studying sketches may very well generate ideas about the piece. Of course one can analyze without recourse to sketches. But where the sketches are available, it would be foolish to ignore them.[17]

Whether, in fact, Beethoven's sketches generate significant new ideas about a piece remains uncertain. Although the focus of Schachter's study is the analytical potential of the sketches—and one would assume that Schachter chose sketches that maximized this potential—the evidence he cites is somewhat tenuous, and is based on arguably minute details of the piece. Given the nature of the tonal system, it is more likely that our insight will be one of degree; that is, information from the sketches will allow us to perceive or appreciate more fully ideas that were originally suggested by the finished score. Beyond the issues of tonality, we are somewhat thwarted because Beethoven's sketches never overtly clarify, but rather record, his struggle to derive musical ideas. The inner nature of this struggle makes these sketches exquisitely implicit, and our readings of them often highly speculative.

My discussion of Schachter's study suggests some of the problems we encounter when we analyze sketches based on a highly defined but also comprehended system such as tonality. But do we fare better with the opposite situation, that is, with an ambiguous, less well defined system that is also less well understood? Let us consider, for a moment, the finished passage and sketch for a late-nineteenth-century song: the opening of Wolf's "Der Glücksritter" (Example 4).

Composed in September 1888 as one of the last of the *Eichendorff Lieder*, the song features a tonal language in transition: in it there are certainly harmonies and keys, yet the brevity and the harmonic distance between these keys often makes their relation to one another unclear. The opening of the song seems to articulate C major (the key in which the song ends). But the second measure could be implying two keys simultaneously as well as preparing us for the rather abrupt shift to F major at the beginning of the next phrase. The A minor of the second

EXAMPLE 4. "Der Glücksritter," mm. 1–8

measure is just as transitory (and transitional); it leads to an E-major chord that is so clearly tonicized as the goal motion of the first phrase that we might accept it as a key area. Yet this E major is really subsidiary to the C-major/F-major tonality; indeed, it may have been created for its half-step motion (VII♯) to the following F-major chord (Example 5).

Compared with the finished score, Wolf's sketch seems innocuous (Figure 1, and transcription, Example 6). It appears on the same leaf as "Der Schreckenberger," completed three days before, and like many of Wolf's sketches, it consists primarily of the vocal line.[18] In this instance, Wolf has revised what the syllabic stress suggests was the original opening of the song: instead of leading to E major (V of VI), it cadences on D. The melodic line, beginning in the undeleted portion of the sketch, is very close to the final version; the few revisions could be categorized as elaboration (m. 3), or perhaps as a way of emphasizing the text (the word "coy," or "prudish," is emphasized by the juxtaposition of C and G sharp and the increased duration of the C).

Even such a brief sketch, if representative of other Wolf sketches, can tell us a great deal about Wolf's compositional process.[19] Although, like Beethoven, he revised between sketch and final version, Wolf seems much more "on track"; his sketches do not have the harried, almost deranged, appearance of many Beethoven sketches, and the revisions are more often fine tunings than overhauls. Further, the presence of both the vocal line and fragments of the accompaniment suggests that even in very early sketches Wolf was focusing on the interaction of these two components.[20]

In contrast, the analytical landscape before us is practically barren. Although one might expect *some* evidence of how Wolf perceived the relation between these various keys, there is none in his sketch. In fact, the only obvious theoretical conclusion suggested by any of Wolf's sketches that I have studied is that some of his ambiguous harmonies result more from semi-independent melodic strands than from vertical entities, a hypothesis suggested by sketches that show clearly delineated upper and lower voices with tentative or nonexistent inner voices. But surely one could arrive at the same conclusion from the finished score. An obvious example occurs in the return of the main theme in "Der Glücksritter" (mm. 13–14, accompaniment; see Example 7). Here Wolf inverts the melodic motion of the accompaniment in the vocal line, creating a B to E

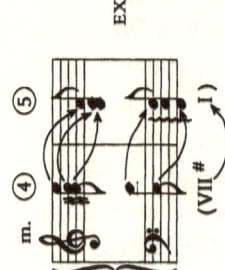

EXAMPLE 5. VII♯–I motion, "Der Glücksritter"

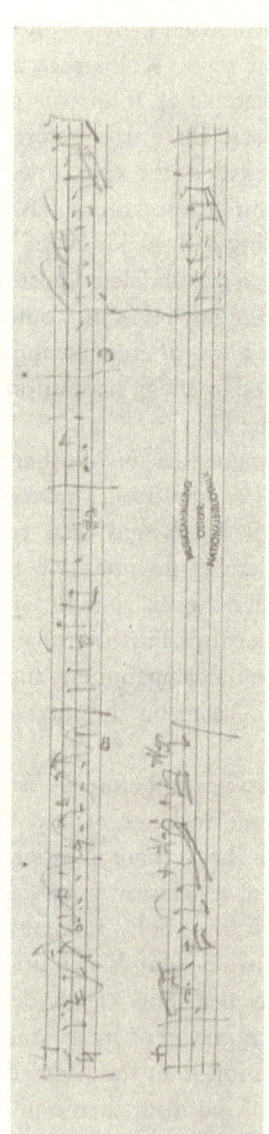

FIGURE 1. Compositional sketch and transcription of the opening "Der Glücksritter." ÖNB Musiksammlung S.m.19573

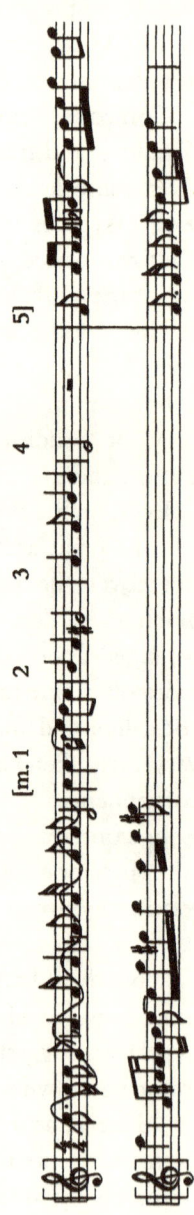

EXAMPLE 6. Transcription of Figure 1

EXAMPLE 7. "Der Glücksritter," mm. 13–14

descent that emphasizes the harmonic goal of that phrase, E major, but also creates the very unlikely verticality B, C, C on the first beat of that gesture. According to Schachter the sketches would then be confirmational, although in this instance we hardly need such confirmation.

We could attribute our lack of analytical evidence to the inexplicit or fragmentary quality of Wolf's sketch. Yet the overriding problem is really the nature of hybrid or transitional compositional systems such as late-nineteenth-century chromaticism or even atonality. When we use sketches for analysis, we are often searching for finite musical relationships: in Schachter's study, how Beethoven elaborates a specific motive; in our Wolf example, the intended relationship between transitory keys. But a transition to another compositional system entails a widening of relationships and a lack of specificity. The relationships that are most ambiguous remain ambiguous, and even if Wolf's sketches were more complete or explicit, we would probably discover little more than we could from the finished score.

All this evidence suggests, then, that sketches are most helpful for highly defined theoretical systems, which, because of their complexity or unapparent relationships, we do not yet fully understand. Berg's serial technique in *Lulu*—and to a great degree his other twelve-tone works—uses such a system, and our understanding of it is furthered by the detail and lucidity of his sketches. In Berg's serial music (and undoubtedly in much twentieth-century music) we come to realize, ironically, that while everything *is* in the printed score, we often fail to perceive or understand its organization.[21] Lost in the complexity of Berg's writing, with its multiple layers, innate dramatic symbolism, and extended twelve-tone techniques, we find in the sketches a mundane but essential road map. Thus, the problem is often one of perception: properties of Berg's music that may be difficult to recognize in the finished score suddenly become obvious when laid out in a sketch.

But how exactly do Berg's sketches clarify the organization of *Lulu*? First, on the most rudimentary level, the sketches often supply order numbers, row forms, transposition levels, and other identifying information. Berg's row technique is so complex that when analyzing passages from *Lulu*, we frequently find ourselves confronted by a maze of possible rows and permutations. We can easily spend hours trying to identify order numbers and row forms (often in vain), or we can look instead at a sketch, where Berg has conveniently labeled them himself. Once we have conquered this basic level of analysis, we can then become analytically more sophisticated or creative.

Second, in his sketches Berg works out in detail compositional ideas that often clarify or augment his statements about his twelve-tone technique. Why, for instance, did Berg feel that the second half of *Lulu* was a palindrome of the first half? What was the technical discovery of row derivation that he reports in a letter to Webern from 1929? Why did he feel that basing the work on a single twelve-tone row assured its unity? What was the "overhaul" he planned once the work was completed? With sketches, chronologically arranged, we are often able to return to the moment of composition, revision, or discovery to investigate more fully the intent of Berg's statements.

Third, the chronological evidence in the sketches can help us to ascertain the exact order in which the parts of this lengthy composition were written. This order, in turn, reveals the evolution of the composer's twelve-tone technique—an evolution that is often hidden when Berg composed nonsequentially or revised early sections of the opera using a later style. In addition, Berg's sketches often reveal both the stimulus for this evolution and the stylistic points of juncture.

Fourth, Berg's sketches present early and intermediary stages that help us to correctly interpret what Berg intended as a primary function of a completed passage. In his sketches, Berg very often works out an idea in a basic form, annotates its function, then performs successive elaborations on it. In the finished score, however, we confront only the elaborated idea. And while its function is often unambiguous (because the passage itself or one of Reich's articles gives us a clue), we sometimes need to examine its initial structure to reaffirm or clarify its meaning.

And finally, the composer's handwriting and his placement of notes on the page often give us valuable clues about the work's organization. This phenomenon has already been explored in Beethoven autograph study; Lockwood, for instance, writes that "Beethoven's musical handwriting ... can be seen as a means of notation whose graphic properties mirror the spatial and organizational properties of their musical contents and even suggest something of their appropriate style of performance."[22]

We have, at best, a tentative hold on Berg's twelve-tone language, and many clues to its organization are obscured by the printed score: motives, carefully separated in Berg's sketches by different staves, become unrecognizable when they are condensed onto a single line; graphically emphasized pitches that hint at tonal or large-scale structures become uncommunicative when they are made uniform.

While the list above suggests that the sketches are most useful in solving analytical problems or establishing theoretical goals, it should be apparent that their chronology is the necessary starting point. For this reason, after I categorize the various sketches in Chapter 1, I present a detailed discussion of compositional chronology derived from the composer's sketches and formerly unavailable correspondence; I use this information in subsequent chapters to treat primarily analytical issues that nonetheless suggest broader theoretical applications. Beginning with Chapter 3, each chapter uses Berg's sketches to resolve a principal controversy or problem that has emerged in the study of *Lulu;* Chapter 3 reveals the dramatic symbolism behind Berg's use of multiple roles and shows how these roles contribute to the large-scale structure of the opera; Chapter 4 focuses on several controversial passages in the Sonata to determine whether, as some theorists claim, they demonstrate the relation between one of the subsidiary rows of the opera and the source row; Chapter 5 reveals Berg's discovery, previously unknown, about his row derivation for *Lulu* and shows how this discovery influenced his compositional style; and Chapter 6 presents a more detailed study of specific aspects of Berg's twelve-tone technique and revises the common view that Berg frequently invoked a free twelve-tone style. The order of these chapters reflects, by necessity, Berg's compositional stages; early chapters concentrate on large-scale features, such as the overall form of scenes, acts, or the opera as a whole, while later chapters explore how these large-scale designs influence Berg's specific style of twelve-tone composition.

Berg's sketches, I have found, can sometimes be as enigmatic as his music; a single sketch may require months of study before its meaning becomes clear. The challenge of deciphering Berg's handwriting partially accounts for these delays; its rapidity and indecipherability always seem, somehow, to increase with the significance of the sketch. In deference to future *Lulu* scholars, I have taken a conservative attitude in transcribing the sketches: I use diplomatic transcriptions accompanied by photographs of the original sketch; I duplicate the spacing and layout of the original sketch as closely as possible; and finally, I reproduce in most instances the entire leaf, even if discussion treats only a small portion. While my conservative approach occasionally produces somewhat tentative readings, replete with question marks, it seems preferable not to risk false readings and subsequent misinterpretations. I have chosen this approach because even though my research focuses on those aspects of the opera that are currently most controversial, I think it likely that these sketches will resolve future controversies that develop from the discoveries presented here.

Chapter 1

Berg's Sketches

Format and Compositional Process

Nearly all the autograph sources for *Lulu* reside in the Musiksammlung of the Österreichische Nationalbibliothek, where they form part of a larger collection, the Alban Berg Nachlass.[1] The autograph sources for *Lulu* constitute seventy-five of the items in Hilmar's catalogue and include materials dating from Berg's early concept of the opera to the orchestration he completed before his death, in December 1935.[2] The majority of these autographs are sketches; that is, they feature the working out of a musical idea before it reached its final form. While Berg arranged some of these sketches in folders or used homemade sketchbooks, the vast majority survive as undated loose leaves lacking chronological arrangement.[3]

In addition to the sketches, the Nationalbibliothek has a wealth of other autograph material relating to *Lulu*, including Berg's copies of *Pandora's Box* and *Erdgeist*, the *Particell* and full score, and a booklet Berg used to learn jazz techniques. While these materials are not sketches per se, they are frequently annotated with sketches and other information that give us important insights into the opera. Furthermore, the *Particell* includes revisions as well as compositional passages that never appear in sketch form in preliminary versions.[4]

A final important source in the Nationalbibliothek is the letters Berg received during the years he composed *Lulu*. These letters often prove more frustrating than enlightening, especially since the absence of Berg's responses reduces apparently critical debates to cryptic monologues. How, for instance, did Berg respond to Adorno's pointed query of March 5, 1935:

And since I'm asking questions, at the close something else that's extremely close to my heart: You mentioned that *Lulu* is supposed to be developed from a *single* twelve-tone row. From Reich's analysis, it seems to me—in at least the Paris scene—that it's not written using twelve-tone technique. That means that you departed from the twelve-tone principle in a central point, and it needs no explanation, what that means. Would you please tell me how it's related? Please, just a card. I wouldn't want to steal your time for any price—which, indeed, should be used for more important things.[5]

Apparently Berg hedged in his answer, for Adorno persists in his next letter, March 10:

I was already familiar with the structure of the Variations that you indicated, from Reich's analysis. What is most crucial to me is the question whether the *rest* of it is written using twelve-tone technique (as was your original intention); or whether, naturally for the most imaginably important reasons, you've been "unorthodox."[6]

Nonetheless, letters such as these occasionally do contain sufficient detail to reveal chronological information as well as innovations in Berg's twelve-tone technique.

To investigate Berg's compositional process—that is, how Berg began the piece and the steps that led to its completion—we first need to classify his sketches, for, depending on their stage of composition, they exhibit a wide variety of formats.[7] Here it proves useful to study the classifications already established for the sketches of other twelve-tone composers. Martha Hyde, in her detailed and complete study of Schoenberg's twelve-tone sketches, cites four categories: row charts, row sketches, compositional sketches, and form tables and charts:

Row tables include sheets that tabulate all transpositions or inversions of a twelve-tone row (or basic set) for a piece. Row sketches can best be described as partial or incomplete row tables. They usually present two or more forms of the basic set, but not all its transpositions or inversions. Compositional sketches, the third category, represent drafts of specific passages in a piece. Unlike row sketches, they have such identifying features as rhythm, pitch, contour, and register.... The final category includes tables and charts in which Schoenberg outlines the form of a section or movement. They have diverse formats but share one common feature: unlike other kinds of sketches they do not use musical notation.[8]

Although these categories are broad enough to classify many of Berg's sketches, there exist intriguing variants that need to be accommodated. In the discussion that follows I comment on these variants and suggest briefly their significance for understanding Berg's compositional process.

Figure 2 shows a row chart in which Berg has listed the twelve transpositions of Alwa's row. At the top right of the sketch he writes "7er Form der Urreihe" (seventh form of the source row), referring to the fact that he has formed Alwa's row by extracting every seventh note from successive repetitions of the source row (Example 8). To the right of each transposition one or more row sketches appear at this same level of transposition. On staff one, for instance, Berg forms four-note chords; to their right he stacks successive segments of the row into dyads. But the row sketch appearing on staff 10, in contrast, is simultaneously a compositional sketch; it features specific durations and register and represents a draft of an actual passage in the opera. Berg even includes its text, from Lulu and Alwa's love scene in Act II, scene 2, "diese Knöchel" (these ankles). This small sketch reveals at least three features of the formats of Berg's sketches. First, different categories of sketch frequently appear together on the same leaf. Thus, Berg did not always work systematically from one stage of sketching to the next; rather, he often launched immediately into compositional sketches upon deriving a row form.[9] Second, apparently the formats of the sketches themselves often represent hybrids, for this sketch clearly features properties of both a row sketch and a compositional sketch. Third, the category compositional sketches needs to be more highly differentiated, for often such sketches feature different stages of composing. The sketch in Figure 2, staff 10, I term a thematic sketch, that is, one that typically includes only the melodic line, or perhaps the melodic line with a simple accompaniment. A second type of compositional sketch features a form of shorthand (Figure 3) that apparently allowed Berg to map out the syllabic stress of the vocal line and/or the general contour of the pitches. The third and final type of

Alwa's Row

Source Row

Berg's Sketches

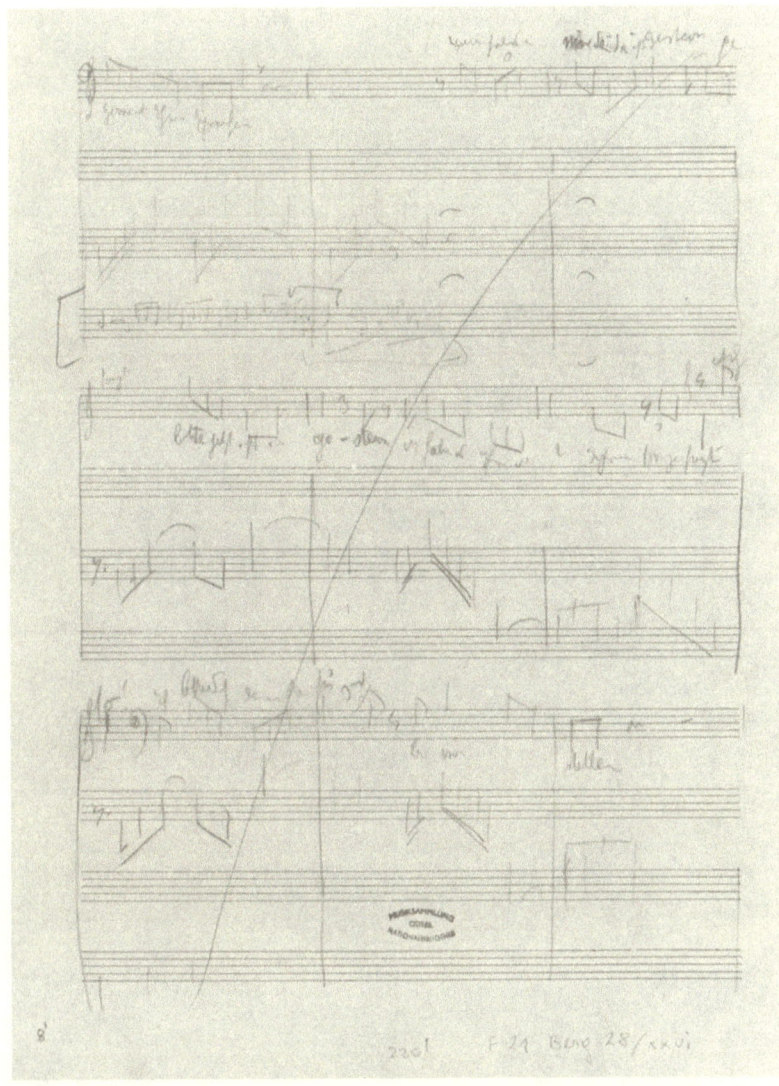

FIGURE 2 (*opposite, above*). Row chart for Alwa's row overlaid with row and compositional sketches. ÖNB Musiksammlung F 21 Berg XVII, fol. 1v

EXAMPLE 8 (*opposite*). Derivation of Alwa's row from the source row

FIGURE 3 (*above*). Compositional sketch (stage 2) featuring shorthand. ÖNB Musiksammlung F 21 Berg 28/XXVI, fol. 8v

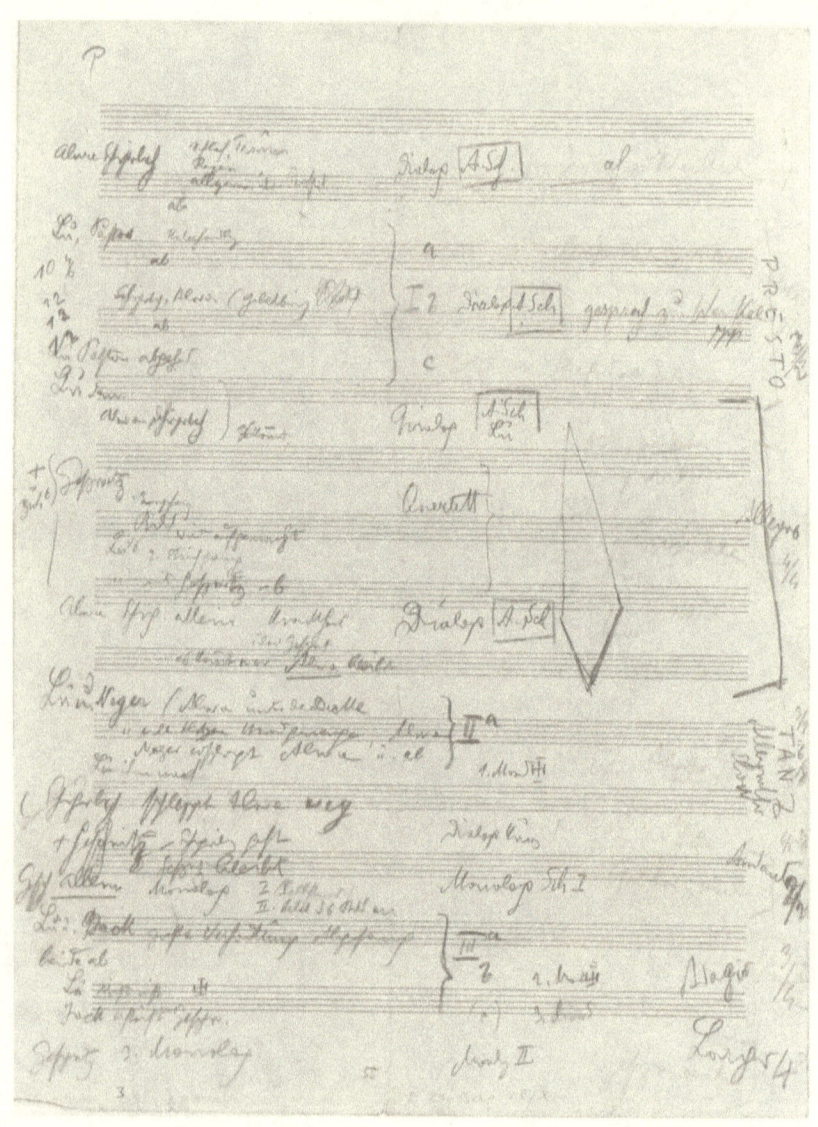

FIGURE 4. Form sketch for Act III, scene 2. ÖNB Musiksammlung F 21 Berg 28/X, fol. 3r

compositional sketch shows the realization of a musical passage; here Berg assigns pitches to these earlier graphic notes and makes the needed additions and revisions.

Form sketches, Hyde's final category, appear with great regularity; in fact, Berg rarely worked out the details of a passage without first completing a diagram or table of its form. Figure 4 shows a form sketch for the final scene of the opera. In the left-hand column Berg lists the characters onstage and briefly sketches their dramatic action. In the center column he begins to make formal and thematic decisions that emphasize the succession of characters; he writes, for instance, "Dialog Alwa Schigolch" in three different locations where he will eventually use similar music. In the right-hand column he notes the tempi and meter that will occur in each of the sections; they indicate that the scene is structured as a large-scale ritardando—from the presto of the opening to the largo of Geschwitz's final monologue.

In this sketch Berg uses the entrance of characters to determine the form of a single scene; however, sketches also exist that show him using this same device to determine the overall symmetry of the opera. This symmetry is his purpose when he uses multiple roles—that is, when a single performer plays more than one part. Chapter 3 looks at sketches of this type in some detail.

Meter, another parameter sometimes not involving pitch, is often a predominant feature of Berg's form sketches. Figure 5, for instance, shows a form sketch in which Berg maps out the different metronome markings of the gavotte of the Sonata and develops metric modulations between the tempi. Figure 6 is one of several form sketches Berg made for the Monorhythmica of Act I, scene 2. In the sketch he lists the eighteen sections of the first half of the Monorhythmica with Roman numerals and assigns a metronome marking to each section.

Two further categories of sketch not discussed by Hyde are useful in classifying Berg's sketches for *Lulu:* the concept sketch and the sketch of dramatic symbolism. Concept sketches, sometimes headed by the word "Ideen" (ideas), are fragmentary and highly preliminary, often showing Berg's initial thoughts about some feature of a passage or extended section of the opera. Their appearance can best be described as an almost illegible "stream of consciousness," as if Berg were freely experimenting with ideas before beginning the arduous process of realization and

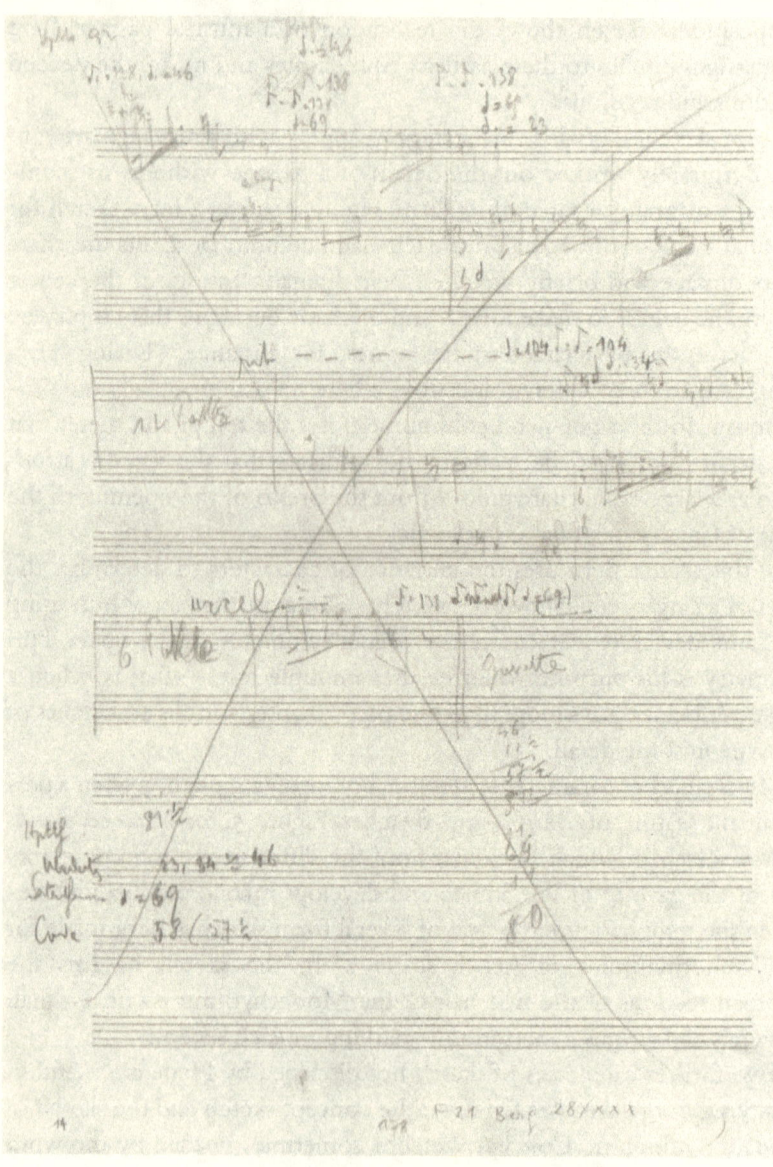

FIGURE 5. Form sketch of the gavotte (Act I, scene 2). ÖNB Musiksammlung F 21 Berg 28/XXX, fol. 14r

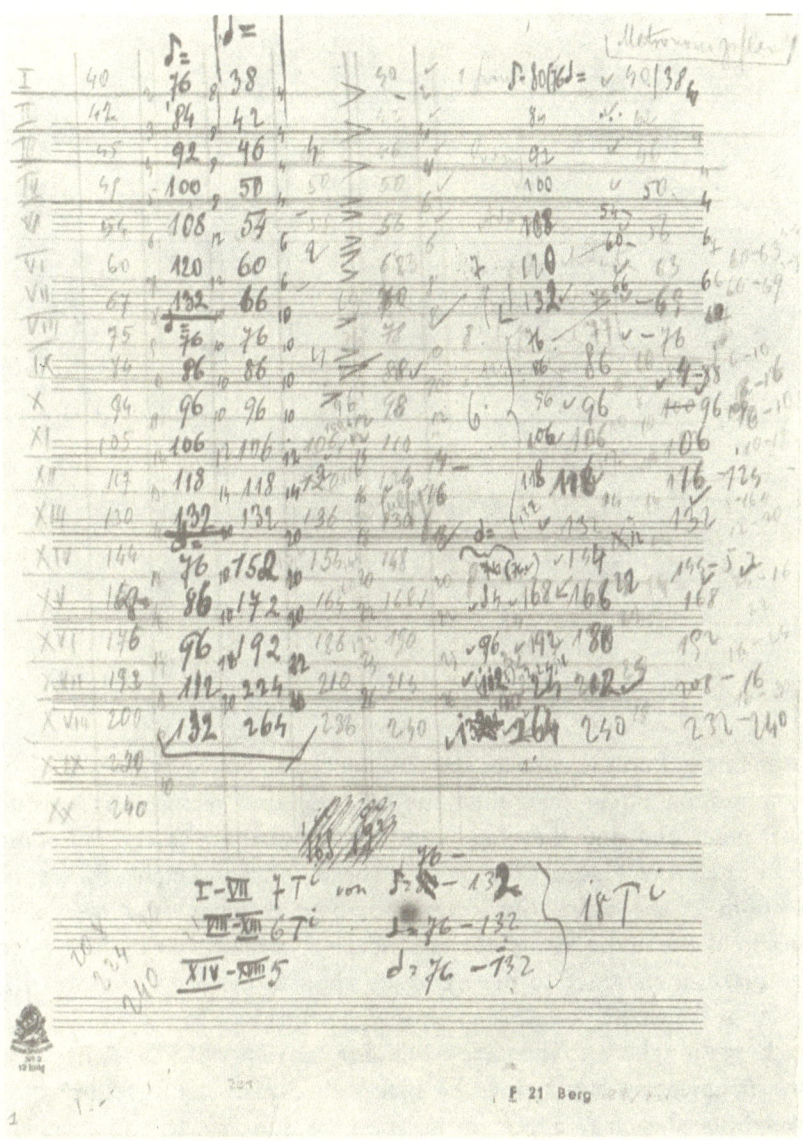

FIGURE 6. Form sketch of the Monorhythmica. ÖNB Musiksammlung F 21 Berg 28/XIV, fol. 1r

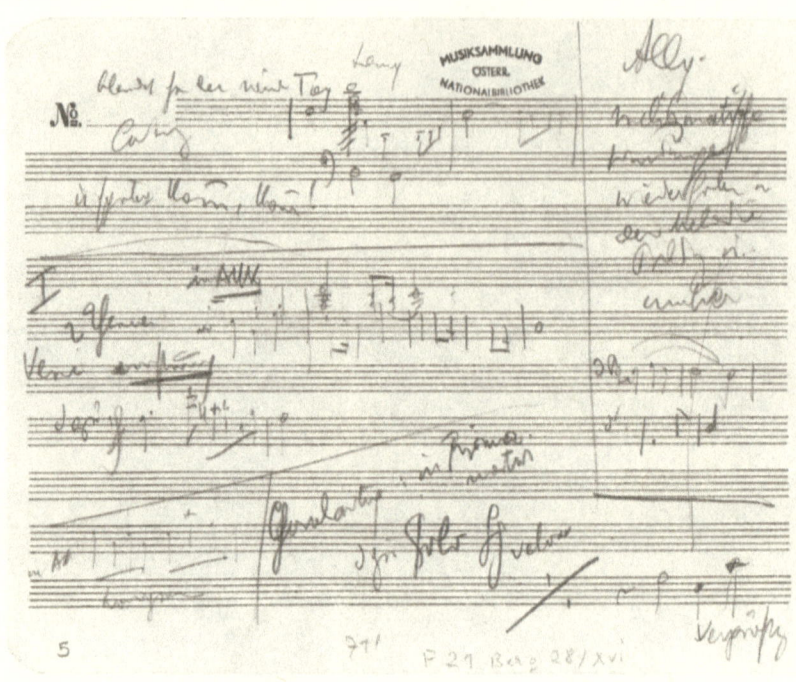

FIGURE 7. Concept sketches. ÖNB Musiksammlung F 21 Berg 28/XVI, fol. 5r

refinement. Because concept sketches are characterized by their stage of composition rather than their subject, they may feature any musical parameter, and thus they may intersect or overlap with the preceding four categories. Figure 7, for instance, shows concept sketches for several sections of the opera. On staves 4–7, Berg sketches what eventually becomes one of the themes for Act I, scene 2. In the center of staves 8–10 he makes a reference to the Marquis's chorale variations from Act III, scene 1, which, he notes, are to be accompanied by a solo violin.

Berg's insights into dramatic symbolism are sometimes subsumed into the fragmentary annotations he makes to explain some feature of a sketch; or they may appear in isolation, constituting an entire sketch. Moreover, they often appear at very early stages of sketching, thereby suggesting that in some sense they generate the passage. Indeed, they often do prove the "raison d'être" of the music. We probably hear the dramatic changes in orchestration in the interlude between scenes 1 and 2 of Act III, as well as the accompanying gradual dissolution of tonality, but until we realize that this "turned-around Bolero" (as Berg called it) is a metaphor for Lulu's surroundings—from the "false glitter" of Act III, scene 1, to the poverty of the following scene, where she experiences her "deepest humiliation"—then much of the dramatic sense of the music is lost on us.[10] The sketch of dramatic symbolism shown in Figure 8, from a booklet containing many such sketches, reveals that each theme of the Rondo represents a different facet of Alwa's character. Berg notes that theme A portrays Alwa as "editor, professional, Schön's son"; theme B, as "artist"; and theme C, as "lover." Directly below the sketch Berg seems to experiment with a different ordering, for here theme A represents Alwa as lover; theme B, as editor; and theme C, as artist, to which Berg adds, "composer of *Wozzeck*."

With this brief classification of the various formats of Berg's sketches, we can begin to arrange the sketches sequentially and thus define more clearly Berg's compositional process. As I have noted above, Berg's row sketches are characterized by a high degree of experimentation. He often investigates the intervallic properties of the row, the row's relation to ones previously derived, new configurations of the row (stacked tetrachords, and so forth), and, finally, possible themes for specific passages of the opera. Once Berg began composing a passage (as opposed to experimenting with these various ideas), his compositional process frequently consisted of four stages: (1) arranging the text to accommodate a particular musical form; (2) sketching the principal themes; (3) setting of text and partial sketching of a musical passage; and (4) filling out the complete texture.

More difficult than ascertaining the sequence of these various stages is determining their function in Berg's compositional process. Confronted, as we are, with so many stages of writing, we might assume that through them Berg solved the problems of the complexity and length of his opera. Thus, rather than attempt a complete draft of a musical passage, which he would then progressively refine, Berg constructed his music by systematically layering one parameter over another. This method gains significance when we realize that these added parameters build upon and elaborate, but rarely negate, earlier versions of a musical passage or idea. A common criticism of sketch study, that it is based on rejected material not pertaining to the final version, does not seem valid in Berg's case. Furthermore, the conspicuous lack of immediate revision in Berg's

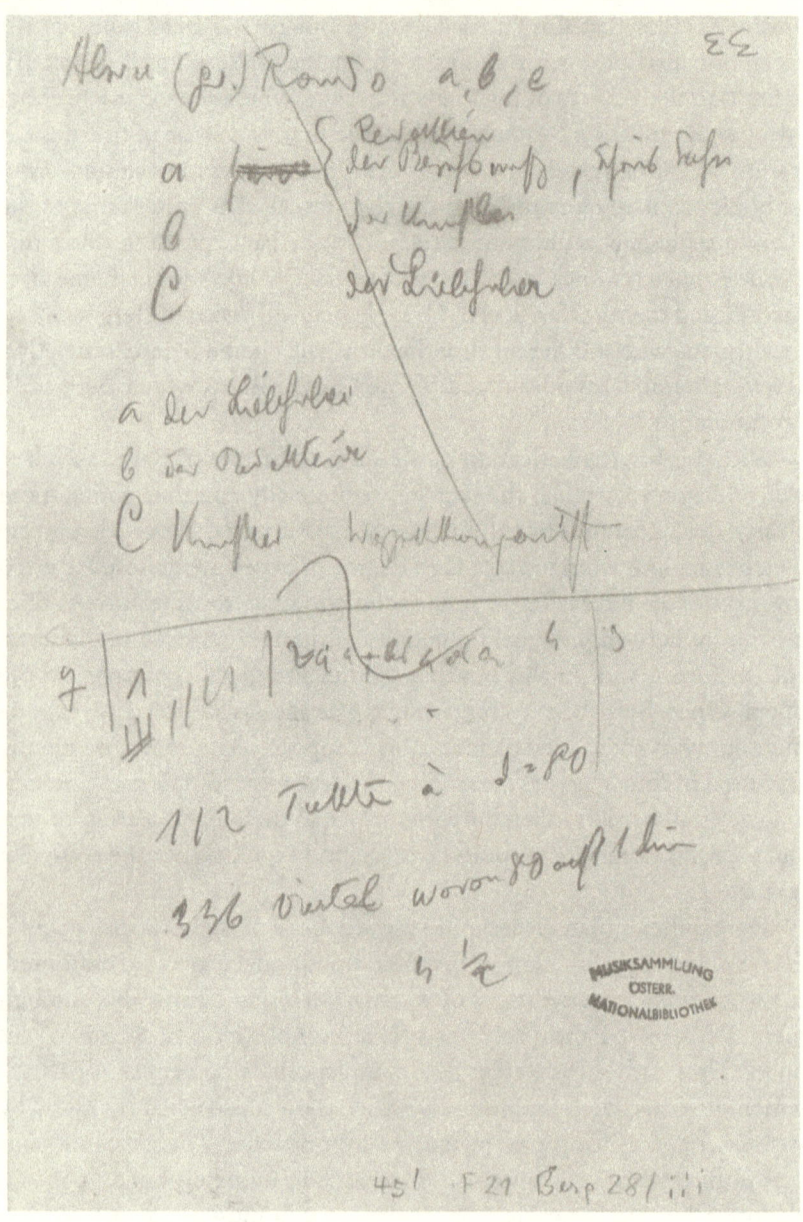

FIGURE 8. Sketch of dramatic symbolism. ÖNB Musiksammlung F 21 Berg 28/III, fol. 33r

sketches suggests that this method of composing was effective, although (as Hilmar notes) it is also possible that Berg was simply solving his compositional problems at the piano rather than on paper.[11]

Berg's systematic layering of musical parameters also allows us, at times, to discover what appears to be the generating idea of a passage, or perhaps to discern when a specific parameter was inserted into the work.[12] For instance, sometimes the syllabic accent of a few words provided the source of a rhythm used throughout an extended passage. One example is found in Berg's setting of the word "Befehlen" (At your service), which opens Act I, scene 2, to the following rhythm: ♪ ♫. In that he uses this rhythm extensively throughout the whole duet, it functions to unify a passage spanning forty-eight measures.[13] Ideas for orchestration, which, according to Berg's letters, was his last stage of composing, appear in his earliest concept sketches and, indeed, seem to determine many of the musical motives he selects.[14] And despite his detailed investigations of interval content, many of Berg's rows were, ironically, inspired by numerical procedures that he believed unified them with the source row. I look at sketches pertaining to row derivation that illustrate these numerical procedures in Chapter 5.

With this preliminary discussion of the more typical formats of Berg's sketches and their relation to his compositional process, we can commence a detailed study of the chronology of the sketches. Beginning in Chapter 3, I use these findings on chronology to solve various theoretical issues and to elaborate on the features of Berg's compositional process presented in this chapter.

Chapter 2

Chronology of the Autograph Sources

Although Berg meticulously dated all his correspondence, only rarely did he date his sketches; thus, to ascertain their chronology is to enter a labyrinth from which one may not easily return. Aside from the fact that only two out of approximately seven hundred leaves bear complete dates, sketches from different periods of composition are usually mixed together in various folders.[1] Further, some single leaves show sketches from different years. And finally, Berg did not compose the opera entirely consecutively. His correspondence reveals that he composed the Prologue last, but his sketches show that in the main body of the opera he sometimes skipped from section to section.[2]

Earlier work on the sketches for *Lulu* has only led us further astray. Rosemary Hilmar does discuss dates, drafts of letters, and other chronological evidence appearing in the sketches, but she frequently misreads this evidence or interprets it incorrectly. For instance, she identifies as a draft of a letter for Max Ast from 1930 one that is actually to Schoenberg from September 1931, and she assumes that all row charts for *Lulu* date from Berg's initial work on the opera in 1927, when in fact he worked out most of them two or more years later.[3]

The purpose of this chapter, then, is to determine the chronology of Berg's sketches as far as is presently possible, given their lack of dates and state of disarray. Since evidence that clarifies chronology is often linked with events in Berg's life, this chapter focuses on these events during the years Berg composed *Lulu*. Before I begin this discussion, however, I outline the general techniques I have used to date Berg's sketches.

Besides evidence from the sketches, our most reliable source for determining chronology is Berg's correspondence—mostly to Webern or Schoenberg—in which he reports his slow but steady progress on the opera. These progress reports are not especially detailed or frequent, but they do provide a general framework for the beginning and completion of Berg's work on major sections. Our quest now is to use this framework, in conjunction with other evidence, to assign dates to individual sketches. By this time, watermarks—a resource often relied upon in the dating of eighteenth- and early-nineteenth-century manuscripts—are of no help. But there are at least four other types of evidence that can be useful. First, Berg had the fortunate habit of drafting letters on his sketches in the midst of composing. A few of these drafts are dated; others can easily be dated by their content.[4]

Second, one can sometimes recognize the year of composition from Berg's technique of sketching. He often labeled early sketches (1928–29) meticulously, with transposition levels, operations (retrograde, inversion, and so forth), and occasionally the method by which he derived a row from the source row; he seems to have relaxed this procedure in later years, although one can still find certain passages marked with order numbers.

Third, if one catalogues the various types of paper Berg used for all the sketches, it is sometimes possible to determine which he used during a particular period. For instance, Berg used twelve-staff paper almost exclusively in his first two years of writing but gradually switched to fourteen-staff paper beginning in 1930.[5] (While such evidence alone may be inconclusive, in conjunction with other types it may be quite reliable.) Fourth, as with paper types, it is sometimes possible to connect particular writing implements with a period of composition. This can be done for Berg's use of ink and colored pencils; for instance, annotations using olive green pencil appear only in early sketches.[6]

The above techniques for dating depend on external evidence, that is, evidence drawn from the outward appearance of a sketch.[7] One can, in addition, frequently use internal evidence gleaned by analyzing the sketch's musical content—by which I mean, not simply noting the section of the opera being sketched and linking it with the date of a progress report, but rather observing the style of twelve-tone writing as well. For the technical discoveries Berg made during the seven years he composed *Lulu* often led directly to a change or development in his musical style. Once we determine when these discoveries were made—through correspondence or other methods—we can more easily date sketches that incorporate them.

The techniques I present here rely on trends, and like all trends, they must tolerate exceptions. Dating sketches on a single piece or type of evidence can lead to errors that have far-reaching consequences, especially if the error occurs in an initial stage of study. Clearly, then, the most reliable dating combines as many pieces or types of evidence as possible.

The following section begins my formal study of the sketches' chronology. I divide this discussion into three parts, representing the three stages of Berg's work on the opera and the evolution of his twelve-tone technique.

1927–29

Berg's biographers often note that in 1914, immediately after seeing Georg Büchner's *Woyzeck,* Berg decided to adapt this play for a libretto.[8] In 1926, as Berg searched for the subject of his second opera, he was drawn to several plays and, in contrast to his immediate decision about *Wozzeck,* he spent over a year struggling with which play to use.

By the winter of 1927–28 Berg had narrowed his choice to Hauptmann's *Und Pippa Tanzt!* and Wedekind's double tragedy *Erdgeist* and *Die Büchse der Pandora;* subsequently he sent letters to a few close friends soliciting their advice. To Adorno, for instance, he issues an urgent appeal:

Dear Doctor,

I've decided to begin composing an opera in the coming early summer. I have two plans, from which *one most definitely* will be realized. It is only a question of *which*. To this aim I am asking your advice: It is: either *Und Pippa Tanzt* or *Lulu* (the latter through the joining of *Erdgeist* and *Pandora's Box* to a three-act (6–7 scene) libretto). What do you say to this? Since I definitely will compose one of the two (or possibly both), it is only a decision of *which* of the two (or which first).[9]

Yet one senses in Adorno's response a hesitancy to influence such a personal decision, for he avoids the issue entirely:

Naturally, I watch the development of your opera plans with the greatest anticipation. *Leonce und Lena* seems exceptionally suitable to me; it's composed only by Julius Weissman, that means not at all. But of course *Lulu* would also be very good and if you decided for *Pippa* your decision would save Hauptmann.[10]

As late as April 26, 1928—approximately six weeks before he would leave for the country to begin composing his new opera—Berg reports to Schoenberg that he is planning (although reluctantly) to set *Pippa*:

We already think often of leaving for the country; consequently I'm thinking of my new work with the apprehension I feel before every new project. It will probably be *Pippa*, though Hauptmann's oppressive conditions (including 50% share of the royalties) don't make the work seem very advisable—from the "practical" standpoint.[11]

In fact, Berg's final decision to compose *Lulu* rather than *Pippa* may reflect Hauptmann's difficult financial terms rather than a personal preference. But despite this initial hesitation, he begins to inform friends in the summer of 1928—seemingly without regret—"I am working on (discretion:) *Lulu!*"[12]

Our earliest dated source for *Lulu* is a large row chart constructed from two leaves of forty-eight-staff paper that bears the date July 17, 1927, in its lower right-hand corner.[13] This date mysteriously precedes Berg's decision to compose *Lulu* by about a year; indeed, Carner suggests that Berg originally intended the row chart for *Pippa*.[14] Written in black ink and embellished with red, purple, yellow, orange, turquoise, and olive green colored pencil, the chart lists the twelve possible transpositions of the original and inverted forms of the source row, as well as various transformations. I discuss these transformations in more detail in Chapter 4; in general, however, many of them rearrange the pitches of the source row to produce tonal components, such as scales, triads, thirds, and fourths.

The unusual writing implements and paper of this row chart allow us to date two partial sketches of the chart, completed with the same paper and ink and four of the same colored pencils. (One partial sketch appears as Figure 9.) In addition, there exists what is possibly an earlier sketch

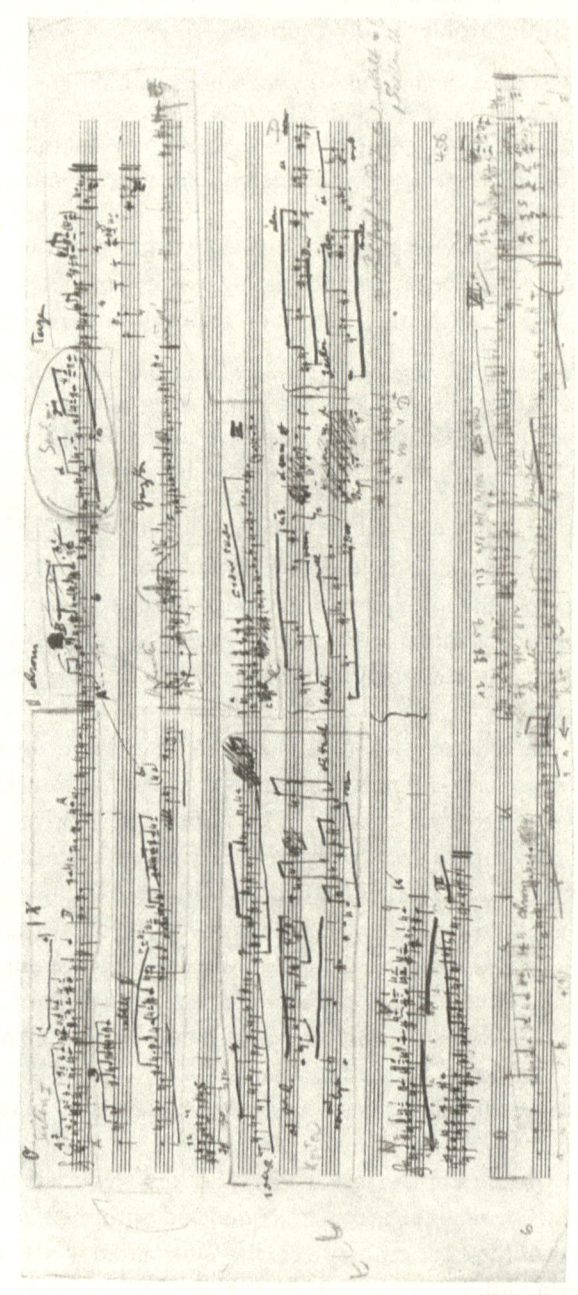

FIGURE 9. Row chart from 1927. ÖNB Musiksammlung F 21 Berg 28/XI, fol. 6r

showing the working out of these transformations.[15] The sketch has dried glue on its back, suggesting that Berg planned at one time to make it, too, into a chart.

Berg waited until the summer of 1928—shortly after he had chosen his libretto—to begin composing the music for his new opera, and a number of sketches can be assigned to this year through either direct or indirect evidence. I look at these sketches in some detail since, like the material from 1927, they provide valuable insights into how Berg began a work of such large proportions.

Our earliest dated source for 1928 is an early, soon abandoned sketch of the Prologue (Figure 10).[16] It bears the date June 23, 1928, in its upper left-hand corner and was thus completed approximately a week after Berg had arrived at Trahütten to begin his summer work.[17] Given Berg's penchant for numerology, it hardly seems coincidental that he chose to sketch the Prologue—the symbolic beginning of a long and no doubt intimidating project—on the twenty-third, his "number of fate."[18] The sketch is perhaps most useful because it allows us to observe certain external features that identify an early dated document: the twelve-staff paper, the almost self-conscious labeling of row forms, the neat appearance and widely spaced arrangement, and the additions in olive green pencil. This tentative profile allows us to identify many undated sketches from this early period.

A small ten-staff sketchbook contains a concept sketch of the Prologue (Figure 11) and other, similarly scrawled, jottings of ideas from the opening of Act I, scene 2, and later acts of the opera.[19] (See, for example, Figure 7, which I cited in Chapter 1 as an example of a concept sketch.) This is our first sample that clearly shows Berg experimenting with ideas from widely separated parts of the opera. In general, the more large-scale his ideas, the further ahead he sketched—although, as I mentioned earlier, he also sometimes worked out details of future sections.

The remaining candidates for this year are, like the notebook, undated, so that we must rely on progress reports and other indirect evidence. One can cite, for instance, Berg's letter to Schoenberg of September 1, in which he reports that he has completed over three hundred measures of the opera.[20] While it might be erroneous to assume that Berg was referring to the first three hundred measures of Act I, scene 1, we can at least begin our search for supporting evidence in the sketches that contain this material.[21]

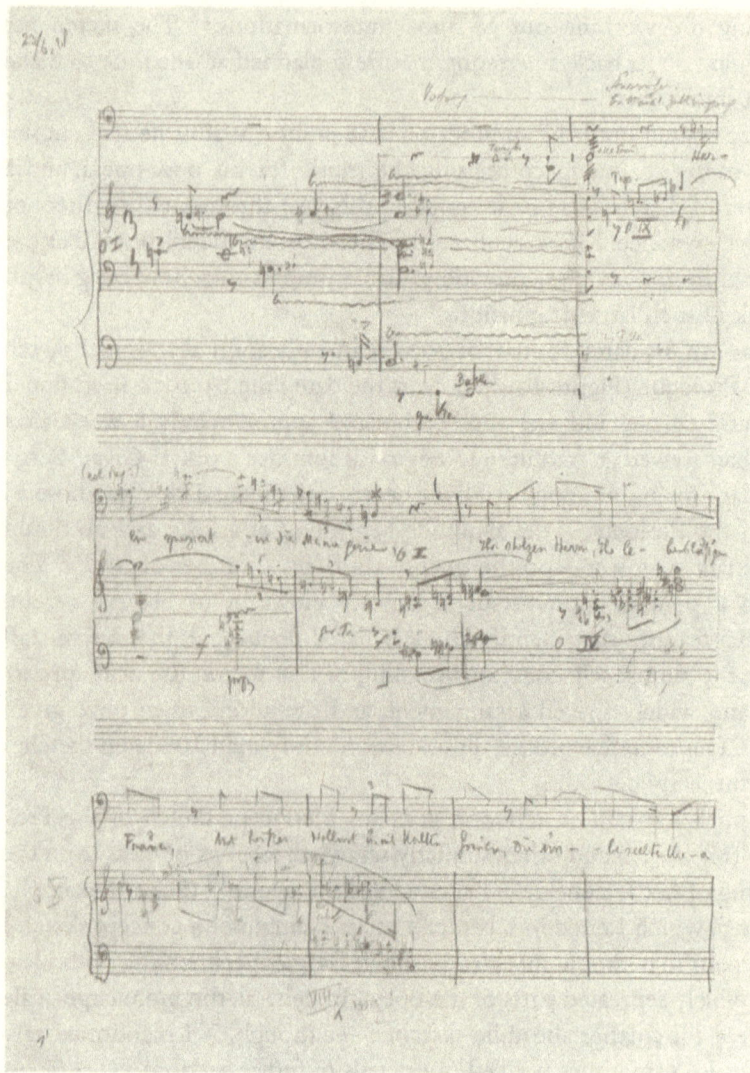

FIGURE 10. Early sketch of the Prologue. ÖNB Musiksammlung F 21 Berg 80/VII, fol. 1v

FIGURE 11. Concept sketch of the Prologue. ÖNB Musiksammlung F 21 Berg 28/XVI, fol. 2r

F 21 Berg 28/XXIV contains compositional sketches of the opera's first three hundred measures.[22] As shown in Figure 12, these sketches exhibit the same characteristics as those noted in the sketch of the Prologue, including the use of twelve-staff paper and the meticulous labeling of row forms. The lack of revision in Berg's sketches, discussed in Chapter 1, is again very apparent, for Berg seems to move directly from one stage of sketch to the next. Here, his intent was to construct a workable draft from which he would derive the *Particell*. A homemade sketchbook (fashioned from twelve-staff paper) contains the only detailed sketches of this material from an earlier stage; it consists mainly of row and thematic sketches.[23] Following the sketches in this notebook are detailed form sketches for later sections of the opera. These form sketches again indicate Berg's tendency to skip ahead to later sections and experiment with large-scale ideas that he may later reject. Figure 13, for instance, shows a form sketch for a sonata exposition (embellished with four shades of colored pencil), which he later abandons.[24]

FIGURE 12. Compositional sketches of Act 1, scene 1. ÖNB Musiksammlung F 21 Berg 28/XXIV, fol. 4r

FIGURE 13. Early form sketch for a sonata exposition. ÖNB Musiksammlung F 21 Berg 80/V, fols. 27v–28r

The final two sources from 1928 were also used during later years of composition. First, there are Berg's well-worn copies of *Erdgeist* and *Pandora's Box,* whose detailed annotations correspond to his compositional sketches, thus making clear that Berg worked back and forth between the two.[25] The second source, a small, gold-edged notebook, is especially problematic to date. Some of its pages have become separated, and they are listed under three call numbers: F 21 Berg 28/III; F 21 Berg 28/VI; and F 21 Berg 80/III. Although it is clear that at one time these pages fitted together, neither the binding nor the content of the sketches allows one to reconstruct the notebook with any certainty. It contains material that Berg probably completed even before he began composing the opera (for instance, a synopsis of the dramatic action of the plays); but there are also numerous sketches for multiple roles that could postdate those reported in a letter to Schoenberg from 1930.[26] I discuss this notebook in more detail in Chapter 3.

When Berg resumed composing in the summer of 1929, the project at hand was not *Lulu* but the soprano aria *Der Wein*. On May 7 Berg writes to Schoenberg about his plans:

Thank heavens the season is coming to an end. In about 2 weeks we are leaving for the country (first to Carinthia). I *must* compose again. I shall probably interrupt my work on *Lulu* in order to carry out a very enticing "commission." Frau Herlinger has requested a lengthy concert aria from me, for which she will give me 5,000 schillings. 2 years of exclusive performance rights.[27]

In another letter to Schoenberg, Berg indicates that he did not resume work on *Lulu* until the beginning of September, allowing him less than a month to compose before his return to Vienna.[28] Although this time was probably too meager for significant gains, Berg nonetheless made an important innovation in row derivation—one that shows very clearly the influence of his previous work, *Der Wein*—that Webern comments on in a letter to Berg dated September 28, 1928:

Your discovery in the area of row construction seems to me of great significance —for the possibility of gaining from the source row, through "*permutation*" (as I believe one calls this type of derivation which you have put forth, in mathematics), rows that are new but *related* to those (of the source row)—in other words, the possibility, for the case when the four basic forms and their transpositions aren't sufficient (as it seemingly is with you), instead of *inventing* new rows, to be

EXAMPLE 9. Derivation of chords from the source row of *Der Wein*

able to *derive* such rows seems to me to be extremely useful for "coherency"; perhaps it is the most advantageous solution to this problem."[29]

Webern's term "permutation" refers to the cyclic rows for *Lulu*—that is, rows formed by systematically extracting pitches from the source row—and one sees the predecessor of these rows in *Der Wein*. As shown in Example 9, Berg forms chords, but not actual rows, by extracting every other note from the source row. The precise chronology of Berg's discovery, as well as its influence on his twelve-tone composition, is discussed in Chapter 5.

There are a number of sketches of cyclic row derivation whose musical content, continuity, and paper type suggest that they were completed at about this same time. A few, in fact, even include sketches for *Der Wein*.[30]

Another influence of *Der Wein* is seen in Berg's use of jazz forms and instrumentation. Apparently the use of jazz idioms did not come easily to Berg, for he resorted to using a "self-help" booklet for jazz entitled "Das Jazzbuch." Its annotations include careful underlining in sections such as "How to orchestrate a jazz band."[31]

How far did Berg get in his remaining four weeks with the actual composition of *Lulu*? Again, since Berg did not date his sketches from this period, we cannot answer this question with absolute certainty. Our most revealing clue is a partial draft of a letter squeezed between compositional sketches for mm. 510–20.[32] The letter contains the date September 30, 1929, which, according to his Tagebuch for that year, was the day he left his summer residence for Vienna. (We know from various letters that Berg did not work on *Lulu* again until the summer of 1930; see, for instance, his letter to Schoenberg from July 22, 1930.)[33] This date is further supported by a concept sketch of that music (Figure 14), in which Berg manipulates the date of the previous day, September 29, 1929, in the upper margin—apparently trying to determine its relation to twenty-three, his number of fate.[34] Although without more documentation we may never know exactly where he interrupted his work, these drafts, as well as their proximity in time to Berg's row discovery, make the opening of the Sonata a reasonable stopping place for the summer of 1929.

The end of the summer marked the completion of a discrete phase in the composition of *Lulu,* for during the previous three years Berg had already determined many of the opera's large-scale ideas: its tone rows, its overall palindromic form, and the forms of later sections. In addition, he had composed a large section of the opera, hypothetically up to the Sonata of Act I, scene 2. This period also shows a distinct shift in his compositional style. First, Berg had begun to derive from numerical operations rows whose tonal properties are chance by-products of these procedures. These rows contrast with the earlier ones, many of which he intentionally constructed to generate tonal properties. In addition, he had begun to assign these rows to specific characters. In the early part of the opera, characters are not exclusively linked to a twelve-tone row; rather, they have various motives that are loosely associated with them. Berg's tentative beginnings in his new style of dramatic association would be further developed in his next period of writing.

1930–32

According to Berg's Tagebuch for 1930, he spent most of the time from July 10 through October 22 at his family's summer home, the Berghof.[35] Rosemary Hilmar notes that the following sketches were originally enclosed in a folder that Berg labeled "Sommer 1930, erledigt" and thus completed during this period: F 21 Berg 28/XXIV, 28/XXVI, 28/XXVII, and 28/XXX.[36] Berg seems, then, to have finally left us a straightforward clue—yet when we examine these sources more closely, we unfortunately learn otherwise. To begin with, many of these sketches show indisputable evidence that Berg completed them around the time of *Der Wein* or earlier. These sketches include, among others, F 28 Berg XXIV, fols. 22v–23r, with its letter draft dated September 30, 1929, and F

FIGURE 14. Concept sketch of mm. 523–32. ÖNB Musiksammlung F 21 Berg 28/XXVIII, fol. 1r

28 Berg XXX, fol. 4r–4v, which shows sketches for *Der Wein* on one side and Berg's hasty derivation of cyclic rows on the other (Figure 15). Furthermore, many other sketches exist, clearly dating from 1930, which Berg did not include in his folder. Hilmar offers the following list, which she bases on similarity in musical content: F 21 Berg 28/XXVIII and 28/XXXI (I discuss later whether these sketches do, in fact, date from 1930). And there are others: for instance, F 28 Berg XXIX contains at least two drafts from 1930 (also discussed later), and F 21 Berg 80/V, fols. 1r–17v and 37r–39v, has preliminary material for many of the sketches

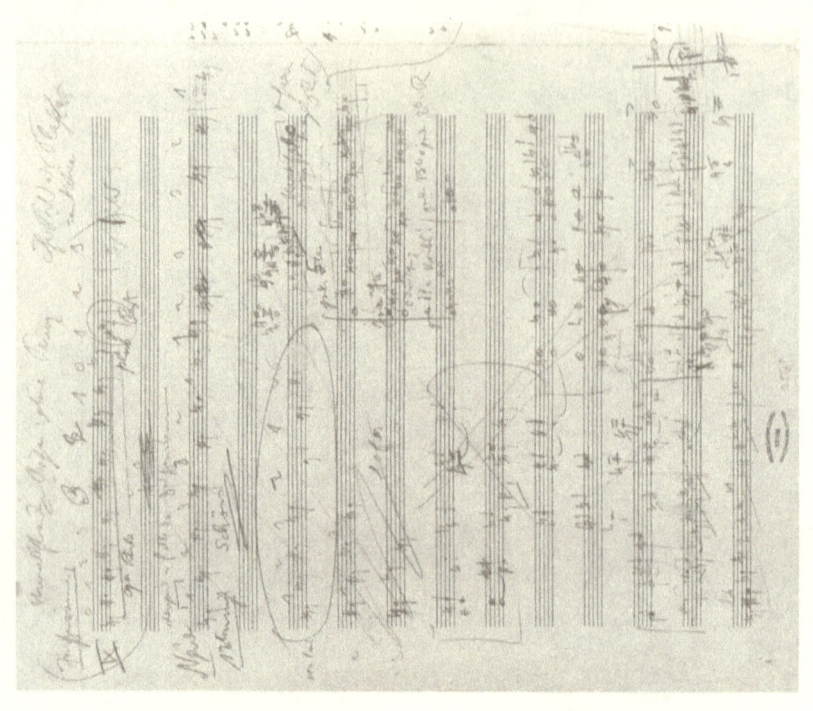

FIGURE 15. Two sketches from 1929 showing the derivation of cyclic rows and compositional sketches for *Der Wein*. ÖNB Musiksammlung F 21 Berg 28/XXX, fol. 4r–4v

from Berg's 1930 folder. In short, we have a complex chronological problem that requires our entire repertoire of dating techniques.

We can begin by extracting those sketches that clearly date from 1928–29 and assessing the general musical content of those that remain. The 1928–29 sketches include those from the opening of the Sonata of Act I, scene 1, to the end of Act I, constituting 828 measures in the final version.

Having proposed a hypothetical boundary for Berg's compositional activity in 1930, I want to consider other evidence that may support or refine this boundary. I begin with the most reliable evidence, drafts and progress reports. As I mentioned earlier, there are at least two drafts among Berg's sketches that unquestionably date from 1930. One of these, shown in Figure 16, contains Berg's draft of an Adolf Loos anagram that was to be published in 1930 as a birthday tribute.[37] Above the anagram are preliminary sketches for the final measures of Act I, scene 2. On the back of this sketch (F 21 Berg 28/XXIX, fol. 13v; Figure 17) is a rather messy, almost unreadable, draft of a letter that congratulates Anna Mahler on her engagement to Paul Zsolnay in 1930.[38] The dating of other drafts in this folder, such as the marks to schillings conversion at the bottom of sketches leading to the coda (Figure 18), is more conjectural. The critical clue here is Berg's note "Aachen," which refers to the premiere of *Wozzeck* in that city on February 21, 1930.[39] The difficulty, of course, is that we have no way of knowing *when* after that date Berg made this sketch. Nonetheless, the more informative drafts identify sections of music written in 1930 and suggest that Berg sketched at least through the Monorhythmica (Act I, scene 2) that summer.

Berg's progress reports from 1930 are perhaps intentionally rather vague and for the most part indicate only his general assessment of how his work is proceeding. On July 22, for instance, he optimistically writes to Schoenberg: "I immediately began working on *Lulu* here—after a ten-month break—and got back into it rather quickly."[40] But only two weeks later, he is suffering from recurring frustration with the twelve-tone method: "Regarding my new opera, I can only tell you that I'm still working on the 1st act. Aside from the composition, the 12-tone style of which still doesn't permit me to work quickly, the libretto slows me down a lot, too."[41] In addition, he frequently reports family crises, illnesses, and other events that impinge upon his work. These range from

FIGURE 16. Sketch overlaid with Adolf Loos anagram. ÖNB Musiksammlung F 21 Berg 28/XXIX, fol. 13r

FIGURE 17. Sketch with a draft of a letter to Anna and Alma Mahler. ÖNB Musiksammlung F 21 Berg 28/XXIX, fol. 13v

FIGURE 18. "Aachen sketch." ÖNB Musiksammlung F 21 Berg 28/XXIX, fol. 7r

the bizarre (his brother-in-law, who suffers from schizophrenia, cuts off the end of his little finger as "a sacrifice") to the more mundane (he enjoys the drives he takes in his newly purchased English Ford).[42]

In contrast, Berg's progress reports from 1931 are unusually specific; he reports to Webern on July 23 that he is working on the development and reprise of the Sonata (Act I, scene 3) and on August 6—two months into his summer work and approximately six weeks before he would return to Vienna—tells him that he has essentially completed the first act.[43] This latter information casts doubt on many sketches from Berg 28/XXX, for this folder includes sketches of the development and reprise and even final sketches of the end of the first act (Figure 19). It is, of course, possible that Berg simply skipped ahead, but more likely it means that these sketches date from 1931.

In 1930 Berg used both twelve- and fourteen-staff paper; he used twelve-staff paper in early sketches of the Sonata, which suggests only that he began composing with twelve-staff paper and then switched later that summer to fourteen-staff paper. Berg's notational style and compositional technique fail to provide additional evidence. One can observe distinct changes from the 1929 sketches, such as the lack of labeling and his use of cyclic rows, but these characteristics continue to appear in later sketches.

A final source that deserves consideration is a homemade sketchbook fashioned from fourteen-staff paper (F 21 Berg 80/V).[44] It contains compositional sketches from the opening of the Sonata through the sextet of Act I, scene 3, as well as preliminary ideas for later acts. If this sketchbook is, in fact, representative of a single summer's work, then Berg might even have sketched through the sextet of the third scene. This hypothesis would support one of the folders Hilmar cites, F 21 Berg 28/XXXI, which contains sketches from this same section of the opera.

Analysis of all these sources suggests, then, that Berg sketched at least from the opening of the Sonata through the end of Act I, scene 2. But with the sketches for Act I, scene 3, we are clearly in the midst of a gray zone for dating. Without more reliable evidence we cannot specify whether these sketches were completed late in the summer of 1930 or early the following summer. Based on the available evidence, the following summary shows the most probable datings for these sketches:

FIGURE 19. Compositional sketches for the conclusion of Act I. ÖNB Musiksammlung F 21 Berg 28/XXX, fol. 26r

F 21 Berg 28/XIV: 1930

F 21 Berg 28/XVII: 1930? plus later additions

F 21 Berg 28/XIX: 1929–30

F 21 Berg 28/XXIV: 1928–29

F 21 Berg 28/XXVI: 1930

F 21 Berg 28/XXVII: 1930

F 21 Berg 28/XXIX: 1930

F 21 Berg 28/XXX, fols. 1r–2v, 4r–4v, 16v: 1929; fol. 3r–3v: 1930; remaining fols.: 1930/31

F 21 Berg 28/XXXI: 1930/31

F 21 Berg 28/XXXII, fols. 1r–2v: 1931

F 21 Berg 80/V, fols. 1r–17v, 37r–39v: 1930

Compared with the sketches from 1930, surrounded by ambiguities, Berg's work during the summer of 1931 is remarkably clearer, for there are numerous progress reports, drafts, and other documents that allow us to date many of these sketches with considerable precision. According to Berg's Tagebuch for 1931, he arrived at the Berghof on June 3 and stayed until September 28.[45] As I mentioned earlier, Berg reports to Webern on July 23 that he is working on the development and reprise of the Sonata, and to Schoenberg on August 6 that he has essentially finished the first act. The date of August 6 is supported by a brief correspondence between Berg and his pupil Julius Schloss that begins with a note on Countess Geschwitz's row chart (Figure 20). Here Berg begins the row chart and asks Schloss to complete it for him according to his specifications. Although this note in itself would not suggest any specific date, Berg's sketches include a completed row chart for Geschwitz that is clearly not in his own handwriting (Figure 21). Furthermore, Schloss writes two letters to Berg, dated August 28 and September 7, the first informing him that the requested row chart is enclosed and the second commenting, "Hopefully you were satisfied with the row chart that I sent on August 28."[46] These letters not only confirm that Berg finished the first act in the late summer but also reveal that the sketches on this chart, consisting of manipulations of Geschwitz's row, were completed after that date.

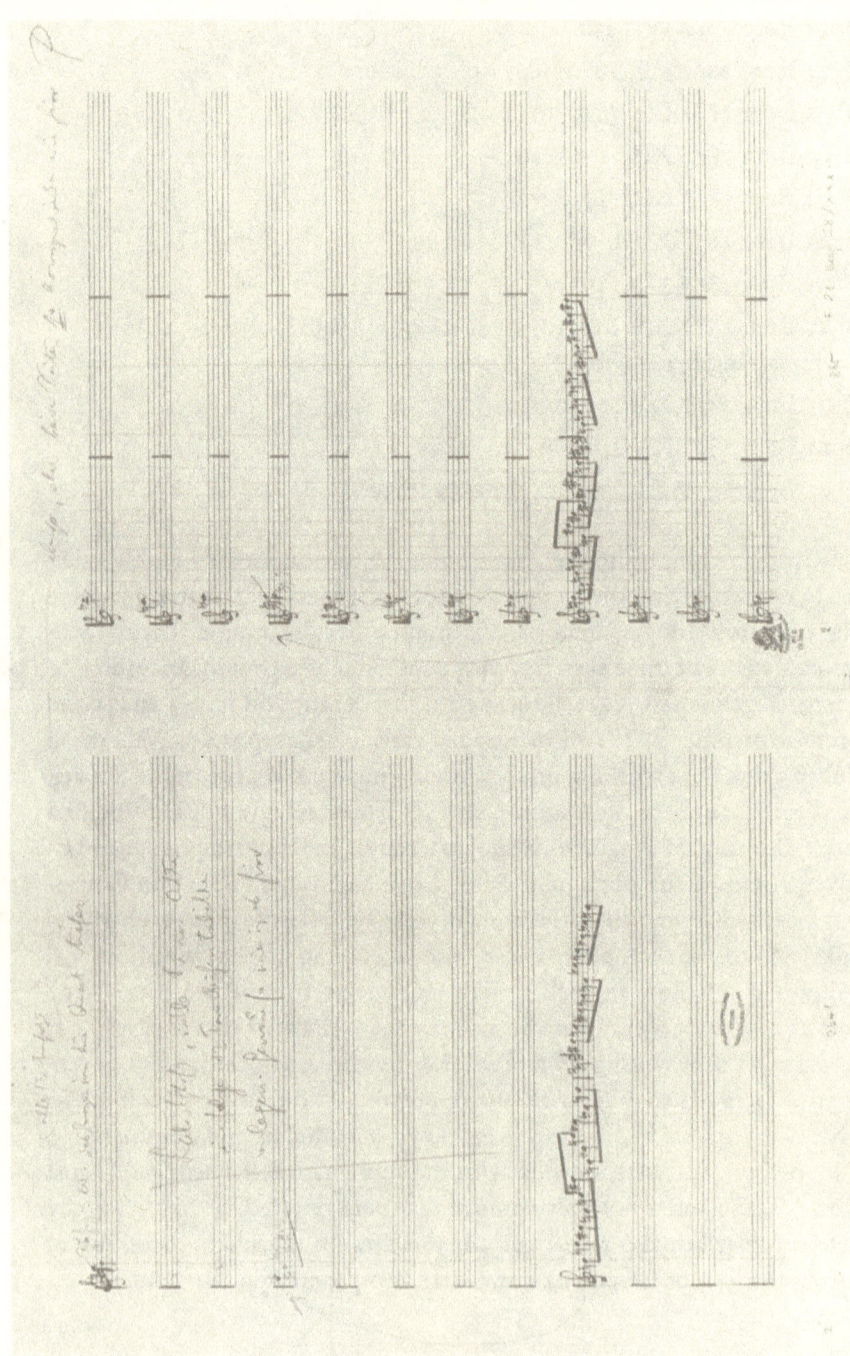

FIGURE 20. Incomplete row chart with a note to Julius Schloss. ÖNB Musiksammlung F 21 Berg 28/XXXII, fols. IV, 2r.

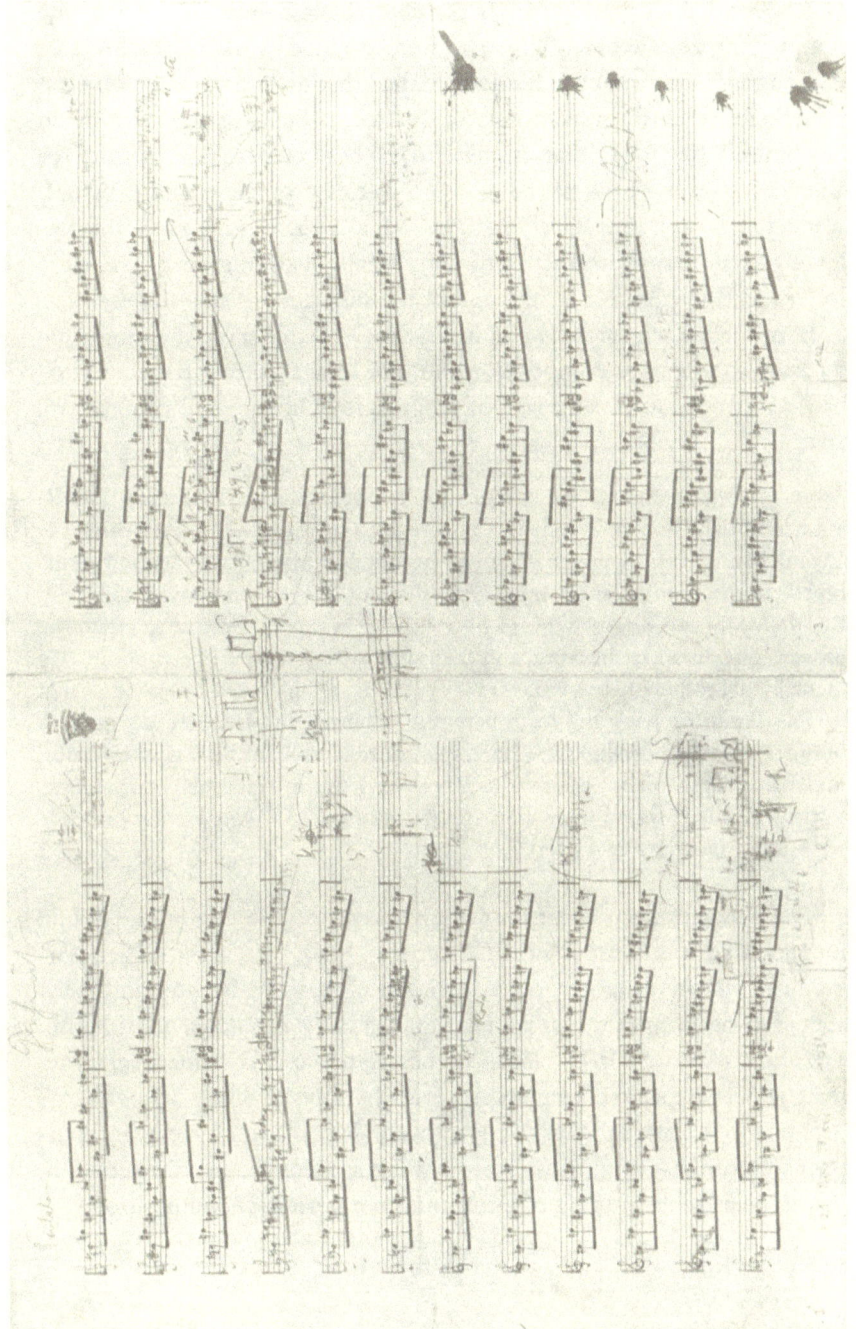

FIGURE 21. Row chart completed by Julius Schloss. ÖNB Musiksammlung F 21 Berg 28/XXI, fols. 2v–3r

A second draft among Berg's sketches, written near the end of the summer, suggests where Berg may have stopped working (Figure 22). Although the letter is even less legible than that to Alma Mahler, one can nonetheless identify it as a draft of a letter to Schoenberg, written on September 19, 1931, that is, nine days before Berg's departure for Vienna.[47] On the back of the draft are sketches for the canon of Act II, scene 1 (m. 174). This letter, then, as well as a draft I discuss in the following section, suggests that Berg was probably working on, or was close to, this section of music by the end of the summer.

Berg's Tagebuch for 1932 and his correspondence show the most time set aside for summer composition thus far: May 15 through early October.[48] Yet Berg laments his lack of progress to Schoenberg on August 26, 1932:

> Again I haven't accomplished as much (on my opera, where I am still in Act II) as I had initially hoped. In June the work was going really well—then came the Vienna Music Festival, which was quite beautiful in many ways; the most beautiful were the 10 minutes of your *Lichtspielmusik* (Webern did a wonderful job!). But then July and August were so hectic that it was very difficult to retain the proper concentration for work, and then only with frequent interruptions. My mentally ill brother-in-law, who was at Trahütten, again caused us a good deal of trouble. We drove back and forth between Trahütten and Berghof any number of times (no mean driving feat either, since it involves "clambering" over almost impassable Alpine passes each way). Whenever I was in Trahütten I got asthma, so finally Helene stayed there alone several times until I would bring her back across the Alps a few days later![49]

The sketches from this summer give us a possible beginning and an inconclusive end. Berg writes "Dorothese Nuria," the name of Schoenberg's newborn daughter, on a form sketch for the Rondo and what appear to be compositional sketches for the *subito tumultuoso* music (mm. 310 and following). Berg crosses certain letters of her name, suggesting that he was experimenting with a musical cipher. Since Schoenberg's daughter was born on May 7, 1932, this draft could not have been completed before that time; most likely it was completed soon after her birth, that is, near the beginning of Berg's summer period of composition.[50]

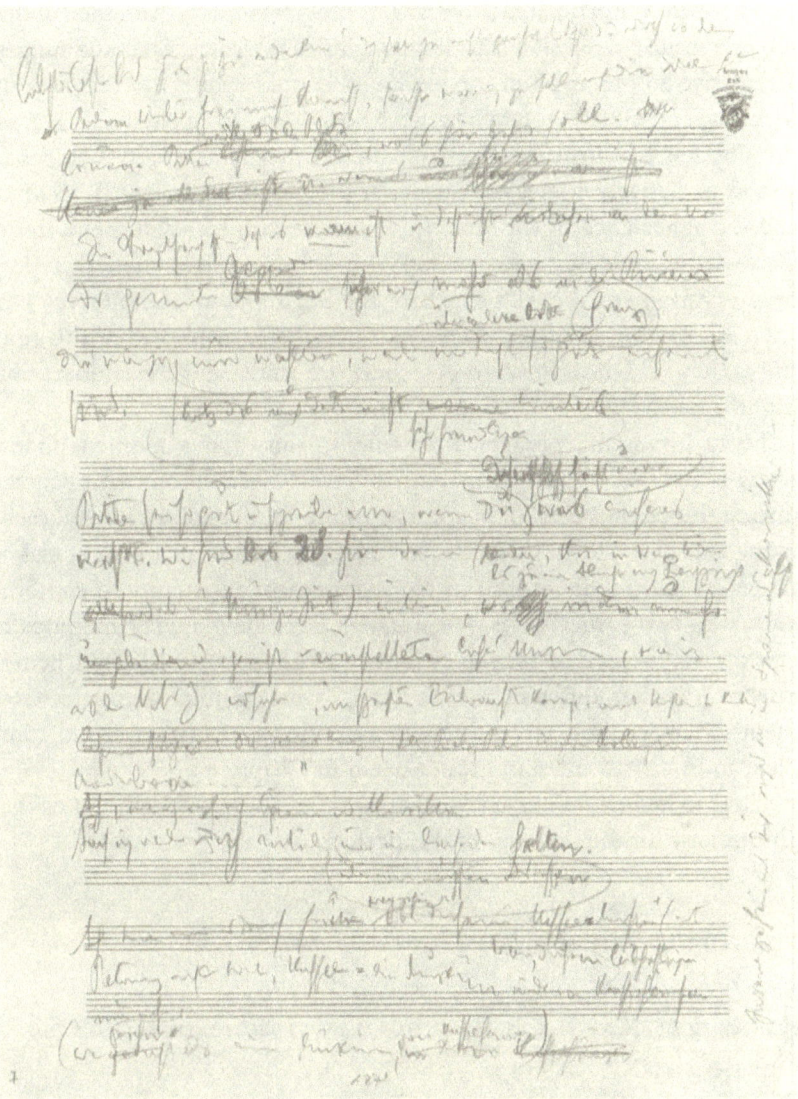

FIGURE 22. Draft of a letter to Schoenberg. ÖNB Musiksammlung F 21 Berg 28/XXXVI, fol. 7r

There are, unfortunately, no drafts or progress reports from the fall that provide similar clues. Based on less conclusive evidence, we could suggest a tentative stopping point, or we could simply group the sketches up to mid-September 1933, when we know Berg completed the second act. The less conclusive evidence includes paper types (Berg switches to almost exclusively twelve-staff paper at the beginning of Act II, scene 2) and the appearance of the sketches themselves (in many of them, Berg's handwriting suddenly becomes very fine). It is possible, then, that Berg began working on Act II, scene 2, at the beginning of summer 1933. In any case, part or all of this scene *must* have been composed at this time since Berg did not finish the second act until mid-September, four months later.[51]

More important, perhaps, than finding this elusive moment in the opera is to assess a change in Berg's twelve-tone method that occurred during this second period. In contrast to the shift in compositional technique that characterizes the first period, there is now an apparent elaboration on his row discoveries of 1929, or perhaps an attempt to combine aspects of two earlier styles. For instance, Berg now applies methods of row derivation used in 1927 to cyclic rows from 1929. In addition, he frequently reorders different row forms to create similar thematic statements. Many of these techniques of composing are both novel and complex, and I discuss them in greater detail in Chapter 6.

The following summary, based on the above evidence, posits a chronology for the sketches of this period:

F 21 Berg 28/XIII: 1932/33

F 21 Berg 28/XXI: 1931

F 21 Berg 28/XXXII, fols. 1v–2r: 1931; 18v: 1929; remaining fols.: 1932

F 21 Berg 28/XXXIV: 1932/33

F 21 Berg 28/XXXV: 1932/33

F 21 Berg 28/XXXVI: 1931

F 21 Berg 28/XXXVII: 1932/33, except fols. 14r–15v and 17r–17v

F 21 Berg 80/VIII, fols. 1r–8v and 10v: 1932/33

1933-35

In 1933 Berg increased his already harried pace, both to complete the opera and to have a source of income from performances. After selling his wife's family estate, Trahütten, Berg was able to purchase the Waldhaus in November 1932, and according to a letter he wrote to Erich Kleiber, he began working there in May 1933.[52] For both "financial and professional reasons," he writes, he would remain there through the winter rather than return to Vienna.

In the final year of composing his opera, Berg addresses his progress reports more often to Webern than to Schoenberg. On August 26, 1933, he writes: "I'm still stuck in the second act: a difficult birth, but I believe ... that I'm now finally on the right path."[53] Approximately two weeks later, on September 15, 1933, he writes: "For a couple of days things weren't going so well. Since then, however, it's gone quite well: I have finally, finally finished the second act."[54]

Other letters from this period indicate not only his progress on the opera, but also the anxiety he suffered as the political situation in Austria deteriorated and he found himself without adequate financial support, labeled a "degenerate composer." He writes to Webern again from the Waldhaus: "Ever since I've been *here*, I can't get rid of the fear that the Nazis will take over here too, that is, our government *won't* be strong enough to stop it."[55] Berg recounts specific deprivations while wintering at the Waldhaus in a letter to Schoenberg from December 6, 1933:

For we are still in this dreary place, surrounded for almost two months now by ice and snow and, aside from my steady work on *Lulu*, encumbered by the petty, pettiest cares of such a life, such as (just to mention a few examples that may illustrate the obvious contrasts between your life and ours:) which farmer has the drier firewood in stock and for how much longer, or whether the water pipe will freeze tonight or whether to take a small auto trip through the winter landscape in order to enjoy the rare bliss of a bathtub (in Klagenfurt or Villach), etc., etc.[56]

In addition to what it reveals of Berg's material situation, this letter helps us to date a draft of another letter appearing in the sketches. That draft, written between sketches of m. 533 and following (Act III, scene 1), concerns

Berg's disagreement about payment with Leo Schiedrowitz, the buyer of his wife's family home. Berg writes in a seemingly exasperated scrawl: "Shall I be even clearer and divulge that it's for these reasons that we've stayed here, where we can live a lot more cheaply than in Vienna. That it's no pleasure to endure this beastly cold, surrounded by ice and snow, with single windows, without a water supply."[57] Obviously written at the height of winter, this letter, its content similar to that of Berg's letter to Schoenberg, was probably written in or around December 1933. This date is confirmed by that of Schiedrowitz's response, January 2, 1934.[58]

In the final five months of composing *Lulu* Berg's progress reports come in a steady stream—no doubt indicating again his relief to be nearing the end of a seemingly endless project. On January 28, 1934, he notifies Webern that he is working on the opera's last scene.[59] Two letters to Helene Berg, written approximately one month later, cite specific passages. On March 4 he writes: "[This letter is] only a note between getting up and starting work, on the way between bed and piano, where the desk stands, inviting me to chat with you, which I would much rather do than get Alwa killed by the Negro."[60] Five days later he writes:

> Worked well on the bus on the way over. (Haven't much feeling really for the character of the Countess Geschwitz, though I must respect her. I find her harder to set to music than all the rest of Lulu's "satellites" put together.) But now at last it looks as though I've found the right notes for both her closing stanzas.[61]

After an interruption of approximately two weeks (during which time Berg was forced to assemble the libretto for Kleiber), he begins composing again and on April 23 reports to Universal Edition that he has finished the opera, except for the Prologue.[62] According to a letter to Webern, he finished the Prologue by June 5, although he notes that he must still "overhaul" the opera and complete a few sections that he had only sketched very quickly.[63] Figure 23 shows a compositional sketch of this later version of the Prologue, while Figure 24 shows a sketch of another section of this Prologue, featuring the graphic notation I discussed in Chapter 1. Figure 24 is, in fact, so lacking in actual pitch notation that it would be difficult to identify, were it not for its proximity to

FIGURE 23. Compositional sketch of the later version of the Prologue (1934). ÖNB Musiksammlung F 21 Berg 28/XXV, fol. 4r

FIGURE 24. Sketch of the later version of the Prologue (1934), featuring graphic notation. ÖNB Musiksammlung F 21 Berg 28/XXV, fol. 3v

the later sketches of the Prologue and Berg's notation of a few key motives and occasional fragments of text. With these sketches of the Prologue, Berg returned to the earliest section of the opera, implementing a new style that had evolved over the past six years.

Although Berg lived a year and a half longer, he of course never finished the orchestration of his opera, and perhaps not even the "overhaul" that he mentions in his letter. First, there was the interruption of the *Lulu Suite,* an unsuccessful attempt to promote performances of *Lulu* in Nazi Germany. And Berg was occupied from late April until mid-August 1935 with the composition of the *Violin Concerto,* written as a memorial to Alma Mahler's daughter Manon Gropius, who died on April 22, 1935, from complications of polio. There is a single sketch of the *Violin Concerto* among Berg's sketches, a row chart (F 21 Berg XVIII, fols. 1v–2r); however, there are many for the *Lulu Suite.* Hilmar lists the following sketches in her catalogue: F 21 Berg 80/VI and F 21 Berg 28/XXXIII.[64] In addition, there are others mixed among the sketches for *Lulu,* including four leaves of program notes that Reich completed for the work's premiere on November 30, 1934.[65]

The effect of this harried and stressful existence on Berg's health is well documented in several sources.[66] Shunning a doctor's care and relying on heavy doses of aspirin to combat fever from an abscess, he was eventually hospitalized with furunculosis on December 17 and died on December 24, 1935, leaving the Partitur orchestrated only through measure 268 of Act III, scene 1.[67] One cannot help remembering his cry: "I must finally be finished!"[68]

This preliminary study has identified important chronological evidence in Berg's sketches and, I hope, has suggested useful techniques for dating Berg's as well as other composers' twentieth-century sketches. I have attempted to strike a balance between oversimplification, and its potential inaccuracy, and a "too cautious" approach that discounts possibly valuable data. It will be possible to establish a more precise and thorough chronology of the sketches when more information becomes available. But given the available reliable evidence, I have resigned myself to the impossibility of dating some sketches; Berg's manner of sketching alone resists such categorization.

The first of my analytical studies, which appears in Chapter 3, concerns Berg's use of multiple roles. I examine early "blueprints" of his plans for such roles to understand the dramatic and formal reasons for his decisions. In the process, I clarify some rather general remarks Berg made about the overall palindromic form of his opera.

Chapter 3

The Interaction of Role and Form

In a letter to Schoenberg dated August 7, 1930, Berg discusses the form of *Lulu*, as it derives from the Wedekind text, and his use of multiple roles—where a single performer plays more than one part. Explaining his plan to join two of Wedekind's plays, Berg writes:

> The orchestral interlude, which in my version *bridges* the gap between the last act of *Erdgeist* and the first of *Büchse der Pandora*, is also the focal point for the whole tragedy and—after the ascent of the opening acts (or scenes)—the descent in the following scenes marks the beginning of the retrograde. (Incidentally: the 4 men who visit Lulu in her attic room are to be portrayed in the opera by the same singers who fall victim to her in the first half of the opera. In reverse order, however.)
>
> That, I believe, is the most interesting dramaturgical aspect I can tell you.[1]

Although Berg eventually reduced these multiple roles from four to three and discarded the strict inverted order of appearance, their primary effects remain the same: they bring forward an idea only latent in the Wedekind text (what Karl Kraus called "the revenge of the world of men"), and they give the opera its symmetrical form through the recapitulation in the last scene of music associated with Lulu's three earlier victims.[2] Beyond these instances, however, Berg's use of multiple roles, either to express other themes in the Wedekind text or to establish a palindromic structure for the work, seems to disappear in the finished score. Berg created other multiple roles—specifically one additional double role and three triple roles—but they are confusing arrays of characters whose members exhibit no apparent dramatic connections and seem not to enforce any palindromic structure. As we now perceive them, these anomalies might suggest that Berg created these remaining multiple roles for convenience, as, indeed, scholars have tended to assume.

But such a hypothesis becomes doubtful in view of Berg's meticulous planning in all other aspects of the opera and his well-known obsessive attention to dramatic detail. Indeed, it seems more likely that we are simply not yet cognizant of Berg's real reasons for associating these characters. By examining Berg's sketches, however, we can find evidence that reveals his plan. The purpose of this chapter, then, is to show that the multiple roles that remain represent, not a convenient device, but a highly sophisticated adaptation of the Wedekind text that Berg fashioned to achieve specific dramatic and formal consequences. I argue further that the techniques Berg used to associate characters in these multiple roles are exactly the same as those he used in the double roles he discusses in his letter to Schoenberg. Berg's sketches of his earliest ideas on those double roles as well as those he indicated for the finished score not only demonstrate these techniques vividly but also provide fascinating documentation for the development of Berg's ideas on multiple roles. I begin this chapter, therefore, with an overview of this evolution, using sketches to illustrate its various stages.

Berg's earliest ideas on multiple roles appear in the small gold-edged booklet discussed briefly in Chapter 2.[3] As I note there, although much of its content replicates as well as elaborates ideas discussed in Berg's letter to Schoenberg from 1930, at least part of the booklet was written two years earlier.[4] In addition to a nearly complete outline of the dramatic action for *Erdgeist* and *Pandora's Box,* the booklet includes many revealing notes about the symbolism behind sections of the opera and about the opera's overall form. These notes are written in a very fast, almost indecipherable, hand, as if Berg perhaps were responding quickly to his own creative inspiration. Figure 25, and its transcription in Example 10, for instance, show one of several outlines Berg made for the opera's large-scale form. As in his letter to Schoenberg, he is showing how the acts and scenes in *Lulu* derive from the acts of Wedekind's two plays. The vertical column of Roman numerals represents Berg's scenes for *Lulu,* and the Arabic numerals immediately to the right indicate the corresponding acts in Wedekind's two plays, thus exposing the symmetrical arrangement of the opera that Berg mentions in his letter. His scenes are grouped in two halves, separated by an interlude; the first half of the opera consists of the Prologue, followed by the four acts from *Erdgeist;* the second half consists of the three acts of *Pandora's Box,* followed by an Epilogue. In other sketches of this type, Berg makes frequent mention of the palindromic relation between the two halves. For instance, on one he writes that the second half is a shadow of the first half, but in backward motion;[5] in another he notes: "From here [the middle], the whole opera runs backward."[6] While Berg was working out the large-scale form of *Lulu,* he apparently also began to experiment with the role doublings of Lulu's victims (who appear throughout the first six scenes of the opera) and the clients (who visit her when she is a prostitute in the seventh and final scene). As I note in Chapter 2, while we cannot reconstruct the chronology of these sketches exactly—since age has caused the booklet to fall apart and Berg occasionally removed pages to staple them elsewhere—we nonetheless can trace a gradual evolution from Berg's earliest ideas on these doublings to those that closely resemble the ones he indicated for the finished score.[7] In the discussion that follows I examine these sketches in detail, first, to show this general evolution and, second, to define each of the techniques Berg used to associate characters within a multiple role.

The sketch shown in Figure 26 (see transcription in Example 11) is typical of Berg's early sketches and illustrates his use of predetermined orderings to arrange members within a multiple role. In the upper third of the sketch (the far left-hand column) Berg has listed, in order of their appearance, four of Lulu's victims from the first six scenes of the opera: (1) Dr. Goll, who suffers a stroke in Act I, scene 1, when he discovers Lulu and the Painter together; (2) the Painter, Schwarz, who as Lulu's husband in Act I, scene 2, commits suicide when he learns of Lulu and Schön's secret affair; (3) Dr. Schön, whom Lulu shoots to death in Act II, scene 1; and (4) Rodrigo, the Acrobat, whom Schigolch murders at Lulu's request in Act III, scene 1. Opposite each of these characters is his proposed double, representing one of the clients from the opera's last scene. In this

Interaction of Role and Form 63

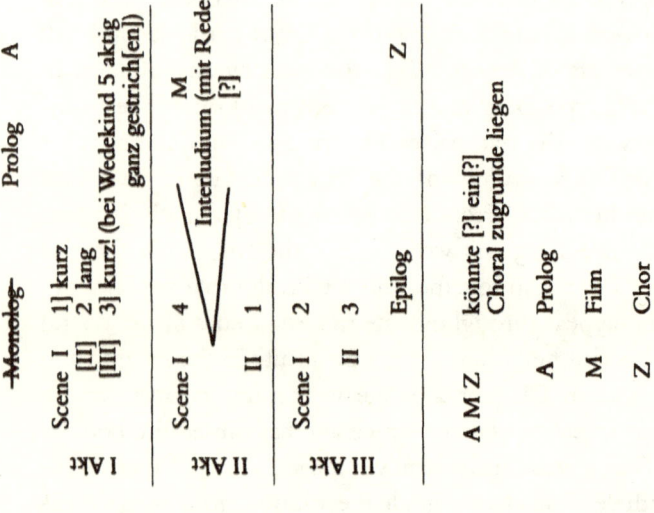

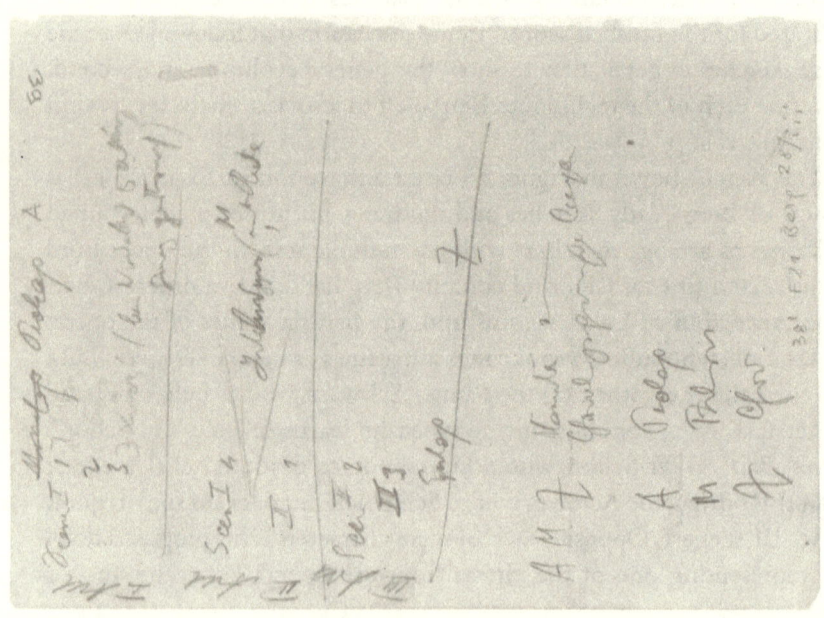

FIGURE 25. Form sketch for *Lulu*. ÖNB Musiksammlung F 21 Berg 28/III, fol. 39r

EXAMPLE 10. Transcription of F 21 Berg 28/III, fol. 39r

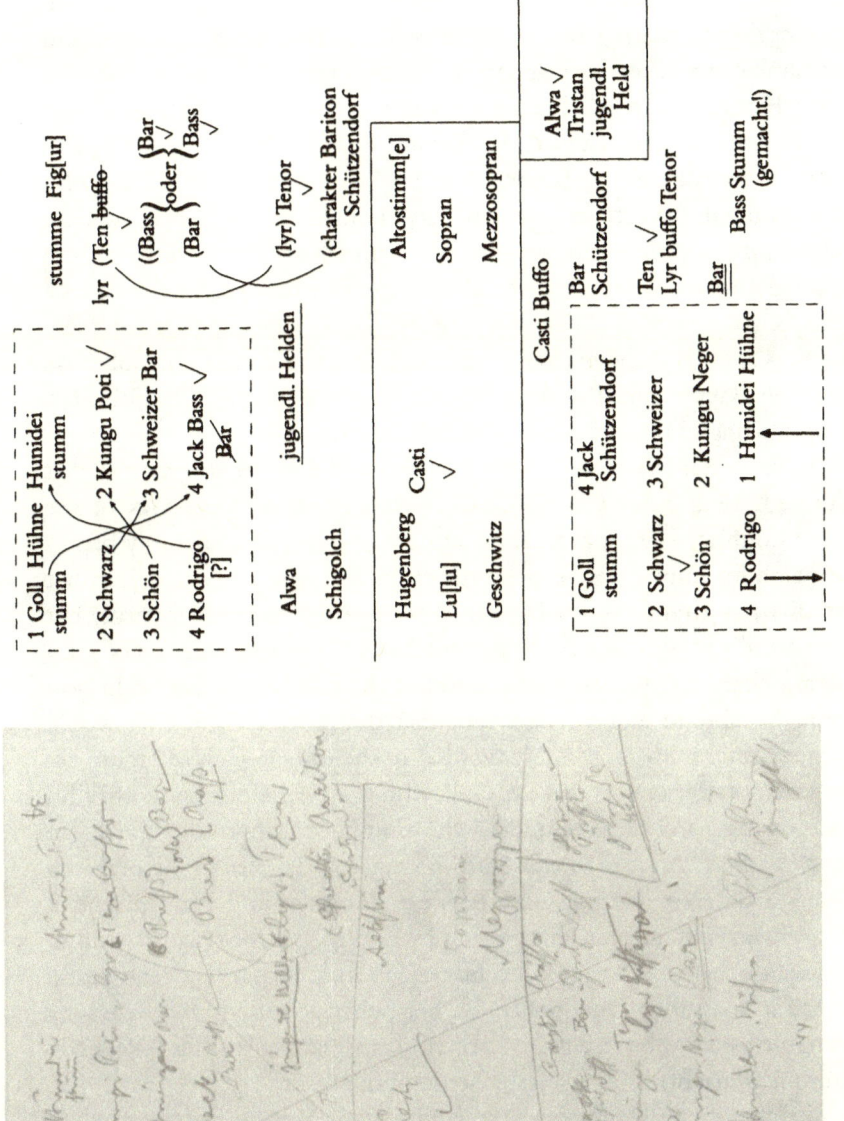

```
                                    stumme Fig[ur]
┌─────────────────────────┐
│ 1 Goll Hühne  Hunidei   │         lyr (Ten buffo
│               stumm     │              ((Bass) ⎫      ⎧Bar ✓
│ 2 Schwarz  ⤬ 2 Kungu Poti ✓│              (Bar)  ⎬ oder ⎨
│ 3 Schön  ⤬   3 Schweizer Bar│            ((Bass) ⎭      ⎩Bass ✓
│ 4 Rodrigo    4 Jack Bass ✓ │         (lyr) Tenor
│    [?]              Bar  │         (charakter Bariton
└─────────────────────────┘         Schützendorf

           jugendl. Helden          Altostimm[e]
Alwa                                Sopran
Schigolch                           Mezzosopran
Hugenberg   Casti
Lu[lu]            ✓                       Casti Buffo    Alwa ✓
Geschwitz                                                Tristan
                                                         jugendl.
                                                         Held
┌─────────────────────────┐         Bar       Alwa ✓
│ 1 Goll  4 Jack          │         Schützendorf
│ stumm  Schützendorf      │         Ten ✓
│ 2 Schwarz  3 Schweizer  │         Lyr buffo Tenor
│       ✓                 │         Bar
│ 3 Schön    2 Kungu Neger│
│        →                │         Bass Stumm
│ 4 Rodrigo  1 Hunidei Hühne│              (gemacht!)
│        →                │
└─────────────────────────┘
```

EXAMPLE 11.   Transcription of F 21 Berg 28/III, fol. 34v

FIGURE 26.   Sketch of "victim/client" pairings, stage 1. ÖNB Musiksammlung F 21 Berg 28/III, fol. 34v

Interaction of Role and Form   65

diagram Berg determines double roles primarily by a parallel rather than a palindromic ordering; that is, the singers who play the victims appear in the same order when they appear as clients. Thus Berg has Dr. Goll play Herr Hunidei (the tall blue-eyed visitor who refuses to speak); has Schwarz, the second victim, play Kungu Poti (the African prince who murders Alwa); has Dr. Schön play the Swiss docent, Dr. Hilti (who speaks only in dialect); and has Rodrigo (Lulu's last victim) play Jack the Ripper, her murderer. Superimposed on this plan with arrows are the pairings that would result if the doublings were arranged in retrograde (that is, palindromic) order, and a more clearly laid out plan for these pairings appears at the bottom of the page. In this diagram, Dr. Goll plays Jack the Ripper; the Painter Schwarz, the Swiss docent Dr. Hilti; Dr. Schön, Kungu Poti; and Rodrigo, Herr Hunidei.

An important feature of both the upper and lower diagrams is that although Berg bases the pairings on predetermined orderings of the client doubles—either parallel or retrograde—he simultaneously begins to search for similarities between the characters who are paired. In other words, he apparently wanted to justify the pairings, not only formally, but dramatically as well. The starting point for this second technique of associating characters was Berg's omission of the first two scenes of *Erdgeist* from the libretto and his discovery that the character Dr. Goll would consequently speak only a few words.[8] In the top diagram of Figure 26, for instance, Berg notes that Dr. Goll, who is a corpse during most of his time onstage, and Herr Hunidei, who simply chooses not to speak, are both "stumm" (mute). In the bottom diagram, the retrograde ordering causes a different pairing, now between Rodrigo and Herr Hunidei. Berg inventively justifies this pairing by noting that Rodrigo is "stumm gemacht": that is, Rodrigo, who blackmails Lulu in Act III, scene 1, and is about to inform the police of her whereabouts, is murdered by Schigolch before he is able to carry out his plan; he is thus "silenced" (stumm gemacht) in the gangster sense of the term.

Sketches completed soon after Figure 26 also make clear that when Berg left the safety of predetermined orderings and began searching instead for dramatic connections, he opened his own Pandora's box. For among all the sketches for *Lulu,* these are among the most tortured, circuitous, and illegible. The sketch shown in Figure 27, whose transcription and translation appear as Examples 12a and 12b, is written in a format similar to that of the previous sketch. In the upper two-thirds of the sketch, Berg largely experiments with pairings formed by a retrograde ordering of the client doubles—although the horizontal lines suggest that he also considered a parallel ordering. In the diagram at the bottom of the page, however, Berg uses for the first time an overall dramatic theme to group together all eight characters, for he notes that with this parallel ordering the doublings represent "Vergeltung" (revenge). In addition, he finds ways to justify the pairings based on this theme, for each of the clients now retaliates in some way for what he experienced as a victim. In the three that I can decipher (reading from top to bottom), Berg writes that Rodrigo, the Acrobat, now paired with Jack the Ripper, "murders because he himself was murdered." The Painter, Schwarz, and Dr. Schön retaliate either by killing Alwa (Kungu Poti) or by railing (Dr. Hilti), for here, as the arrows indicate, Berg is trying to decide between two different pairings.

In contrast to the complexity (and uncertainty) of these sketches, the ones that follow seem suddenly decisive, perhaps even inspired. In the sketch shown in Figure 28, one still sees the careful pairing based on dramatic similarities. Now, however, Berg has dropped the characters Rodrigo and Dr. Hilti, so that the victims are finally confined to the first half of the opera. This decision leads Berg to a final technique of association, this time based on the large-scale symmetry of the opera. Hopkins, the English equivalent of Herr Hunidei in the first edition of *Pandora's Box* (1904), again doubles as the mute Dr. Goll.[9] Schön, as Kungu Poti, kills his son, Alwa, finally resolving the father-son conflict over Lulu that began with the first scene of the opera. But now Berg makes a new connection; he writes "Maler (Messer!)" (painter [knife!]), because the Painter, who commits suicide by slitting his throat with a razor, uses the blade once again as Jack the Ripper to murder Lulu.

From this stage of sketching, it was only a short distance to the doublings Berg indicated for the finished score. For these he again doubles Dr. Goll and the first visitor, Herr Hunidei, but now he switches the doublings of the Painter and Dr. Schön. The Painter is now associated with Kungu Poti, but in a hidden way. Perle notes that Berg may simply be using the Painter's name, Schwarz, to make the connection.[10] Dramatically, however, the doubling of Schön and Jack the Ripper is very strong. The climax of the first half of the opera, Lulu's murder of Dr.

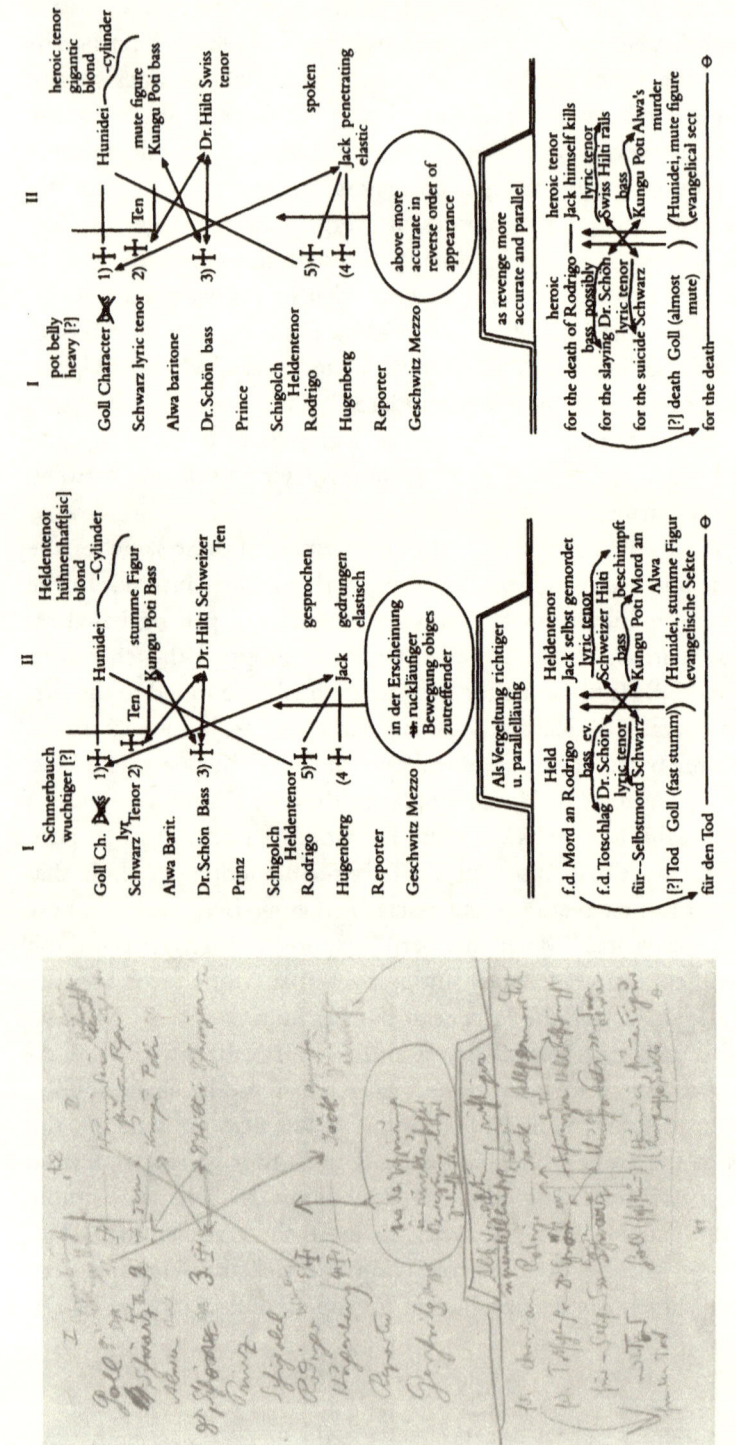

FIGURE 27. Sketch of "victim/client" pairings, stage 2. ÖNB Musiksammlung F 21 Berg 28/III, fol. 37v

EXAMPLE 12A. Transcription of F 21 Berg 28/III, fol. 37v

EXAMPLE 12B. Translation of F 21 Berg 28/III, fol. 37v

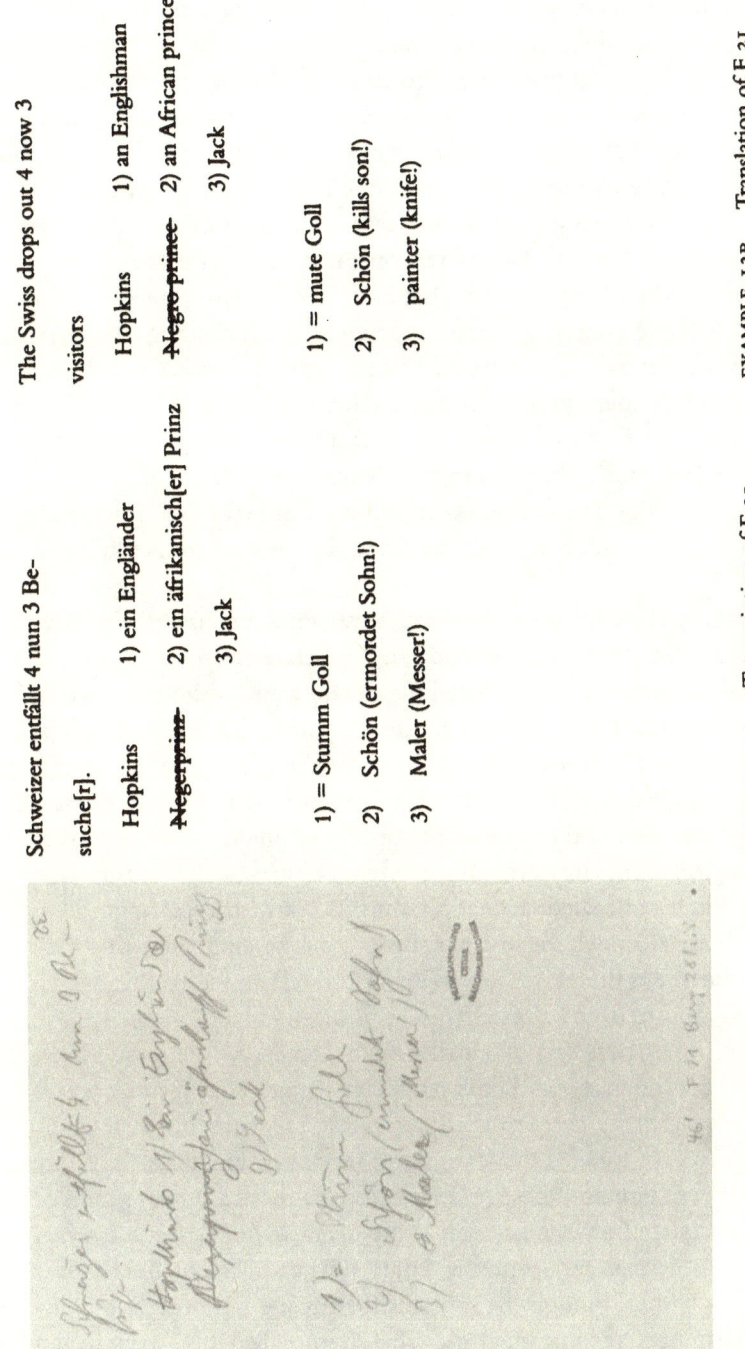

FIGURE 28. Sketch of "victim/client" pairings, stage 3. ÖNB Musiksammlung F 21 Berg 28/III, fol. 32r

Schweizer entfällt 4 nun 3 Be-
suche[r].

Hopkins   1) ein Engländer
~~Negerprinz~~   2) ein afrikanisch[er] Prinz
                 3) Jack

1) = Stumm Goll
2)   Schön (ermordet Sohn!)
3)   Maler (Messer!)

EXAMPLE 13A. Transcription of F 21 Berg 28/III, fol. 32r

The Swiss drops out 4 now 3
visitors

Hopkins   1) an Englishman
~~Negro prince~~   2) an African prince
                 3) Jack

1) = mute Goll
2)   Schön (kills son!)
3)   painter (knife!)

EXAMPLE 13B. Translation of F 21 Berg 28/III, fol. 32r

Interaction of Role and Form   69

Schön, is now matched by the final tragedy of the second half, when Schön, as Jack the Ripper, murders Lulu.

Now that I have identified Berg's techniques of associating characters (as shown through his sketches), let me briefly summarize these techniques and show how they are retained in the finished score. First, Berg associates the three victims and the three clients in a general way through the position of the two groups in the large-scale form of the opera; the victims appear in the first half of the opera, starting with the opening scene, and the clients appear in the last half, specifically in the last scene. Dramatically, Berg associates all six characters with his heading "the retaliation" or "the revenge of the world of men." He further links each pair through either hidden symbolism or dramatic similarities—for instance, both Dr. Goll, the first victim, and the character he doubles, Hunidei, are made mute. And finally, he links each pair through order of appearance: in the last scene the doubles appear in the same order as in the first half, which Perle points out is in itself symbolic, for they are in fact killed in that order.[11]

What these sketches do not reveal, however, is precisely how Berg planned to reflect these subtle associations between characters in the music itself, although a few associations are apparent without the aid of sketches. The music for each client in the last scene is based almost entirely on a recapitulation of his music from the first half of the opera, where he appeared as a victim. Thus we can associate the paired characters in a general way and recognize the opera's symmetrical form. Within these recapitulations, however, Berg often constructs the music so it expresses more concealed dramatic connections. In the pairing of Dr. Goll and Herr Hunidei, for instance, Berg wants to emphasize that they are both mute. He therefore limits Herr Hunidei's music to that which we hear in the first scene after Dr. Goll is dead—and also mute.

At other times Berg sets two analogous sentences to the same music. Perle notes, for instance, that Lulu's remark to Kungu Poti, "I think you're a good-looking man," is set to the same music in which his double, the Painter, remarks to Lulu, "I think you look very charming today."[12] More often, however, Berg uses these recapitulations to recall a similar mood or psychological state from the first half of the opera. In Act II, scene 1, when Dr. Schön, in despair and doubting Lulu's fidelity, pulls out his revolver and searches wildly through the curtains for anyone who might be hiding, we hear him accompanied by what Berg called his "persecution mania" music. When in the final scene, Lulu begs Jack the Ripper to spend the night with her, Jack says, "That sounds suspicious! Someone might go through my pockets!" and we hear the same music again.

It is not in the same booklet but in sketches completed slightly later that Berg reveals the symbolism behind three other multiple roles. I examine these sketches, first, to ascertain their overall dramatic themes and, second, to observe how these dramatic themes interact with the opera's large-scale form. I begin with the triple role involving the Prince, the Manservant, and the Marquis. Musically, Berg makes the relatedness of these characters explicit: they have the same twelve-tone row, formed by extracting notes from successive statements of Alwa's row, the source row, and Dr. Schön's row; their music consists of *Choralbearbeitungen;* and each is represented by a different stringed instrument—the Prince by a cello, the Manservant by the viola, and the Marquis by the violin. Dramatically, however, they seem diverse. The Prince, a rich African explorer who wants to marry Lulu, visits her in her theater dressing room in Act I, scene 3; the Manservant, employed by Dr. Schön, appears in Act II, scene 1; the Marquis, a procurer who is pressuring Lulu into joining a brothel in Cairo, appears in Act III, scene 1. It is only from his sketches that we discover what Berg thought these three characters had in common.

Figure 29 shows a sketch for this triple role. Near its center Berg writes: "retention of the chorale idea and the 'Faithfully led,' whether it be into the slavery of marriage, the household, or the brothel." Berg apparently intends that each of these characters represent a different form of slavery, just as the victims/clients represent the theme "the revenge of the world of men." But a further similarity seems important, for there is a pairing off of members of the group; the Prince and the Marquis are actively leading Lulu into slavery, while the Manservant is merely a passive symbol of it. And then there is the citation in Berg's note, "Treulich geführt," or "Faithfully led," which refers to the wedding march from the third act of *Lohengrin*.[13] The idea of marriage immediately suggests the Prince, and indeed sections of the wedding march occur in his music. Nonetheless, as Berg's sketch makes clear, it is not just this surface aspect of the tune that interests him. In his article on Berg's *Violin Concerto*, Douglas Jarman shows that Berg's borrowed tunes all have an underlying significance, derived from their texts—even though these texts are often omitted.[14] The wedding march begins to appear where the Prince, near the end of his *Choralbearbeitung*, sings: "As a wife she would make a man

| Für II u. III | Konzert[ante] | | For II and III | concert[ante] |

Der Prinz $I_3(h)D-$ as a! ⌐Vcl   The Prince $I_3(h)D-$ $a^b a!$ ⌐cello
Kammerdiener $II_1( )$ { Ten buffo Br   Manservant $II_1( )$ { Ten buffo viola
Mädchenhändler III_1 tiefer (ev. Bar)   Procurer III_1 lower (possibly
                          $\underline{\underline{a}}$ Gg   bar.) violin
                                                                          $\underline{\underline{a}}$

                    Reihe (11 Ton)   row (11-tone)

u. des "Treulich geführt," gleichgültig ob   and the "Faithfully led," whether it be
beibehaltung der Choralidee   retention of the chorale idea

                { Ehe, des   { marriage, the
in die Sclaverei der { Haushalts oder   into the slavery of { household, or
                { des Bordells   { the brothel

Vom gleichen Gesichtspunkt die 3   Treat the three henchmen (of the theater,
Schergen (des Theaters, der Polizei u. der   the police, and finance) in the
Finanz) behandeln!   same manner!

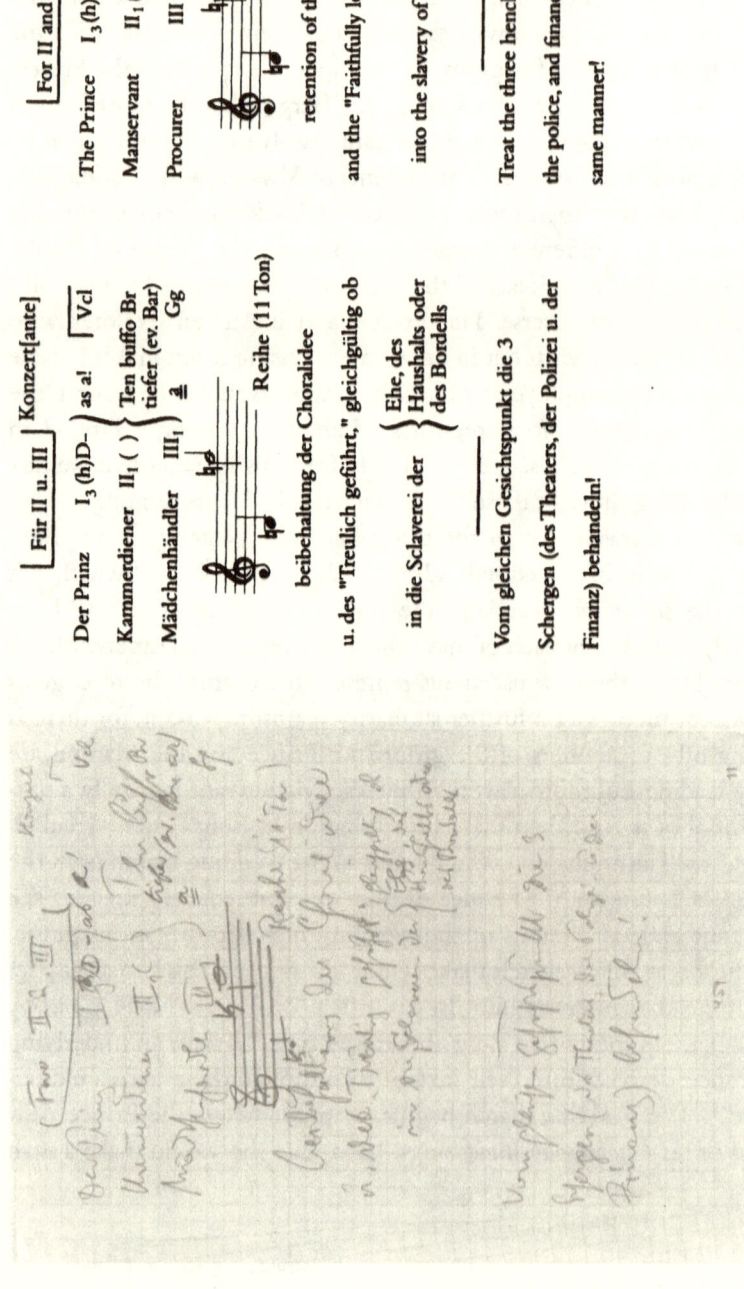

so happy. (As my wife . . .)." If we look at the sketches for the Marquis's chorale variations in Act III, scene 1 (one of which appears as Figure 30), we see that Berg consistently writes "mit Treulich geführt" next to his second chorale variation. (In the sketch it appears directly below the arrow.) This is where the Marquis sings, "But you'll fit all the more perfectly in the position I have sought out for you. I told you that I was a procurer." The message is clear: in both instances Lulu is being "faithfully led" into a type of slavery, and the Marquis and the Prince are merely different sides of the same coin. Berg makes the connection between the Prince and the Marquis explicit with a note in the lower left-hand corner of his sketch. He writes "Treulich geführt, Bordell ist Ehe" (Faithfully led, brothel is marriage).

The inclusion of the wedding march in a procurer's music is a satirical touch we would expect more from Weill than from Berg, and although Berg repeatedly mentions the idea in his sketches, he may have discarded the tune or made it unrecognizable.[15] Other clues, however, make the abusive nature of the Prince and Marquis clear. Friedrich Cerha has questioned whether Berg included the English Waltz in both the Prince's and the Marquis's music to bring out the analogous dramatic situation.[16] When we first hear the English Waltz in Act I, scene 3, it accompanies Lulu's words "he [Dr. Schön] is trying to find someone rich enough to marry me," by which she means that Dr. Schön is, in a sense, selling her into marriage. We hear the English Waltz in Act III, scene 1, at a time when Lulu is being sold into prostitution, for the Marquis will receive 1,200 marks if Lulu goes to work for a brothel in Cairo.

What was Berg's source for the "Bordell ist Ehe" theme? It was probably not Wedekind, who, although he equates marriage and prostitution in other plays, makes no explicit parallel between them in his *Lulu* text. Rather, it seems likely that for the idea behind this pairing, Berg turned once again to Karl Kraus.

In his biography of Berg, Willi Reich cites a line by Kraus as the inspiration for Berg's doubling of the victims and clients: "The great retalia-

FIGURE 29 (*opposite*). Sketch of the triple roles of the Prince, Manservant, Marquis and the Theater Director, Police Commissioner, Banker. ÖNB Musiksammlung F 21 Berg 28/VI, fol. 11r

EXAMPLES 14A AND 14B (*opposite*). Transcription and translation of F 21 Berg 28/VI, fol. 11r

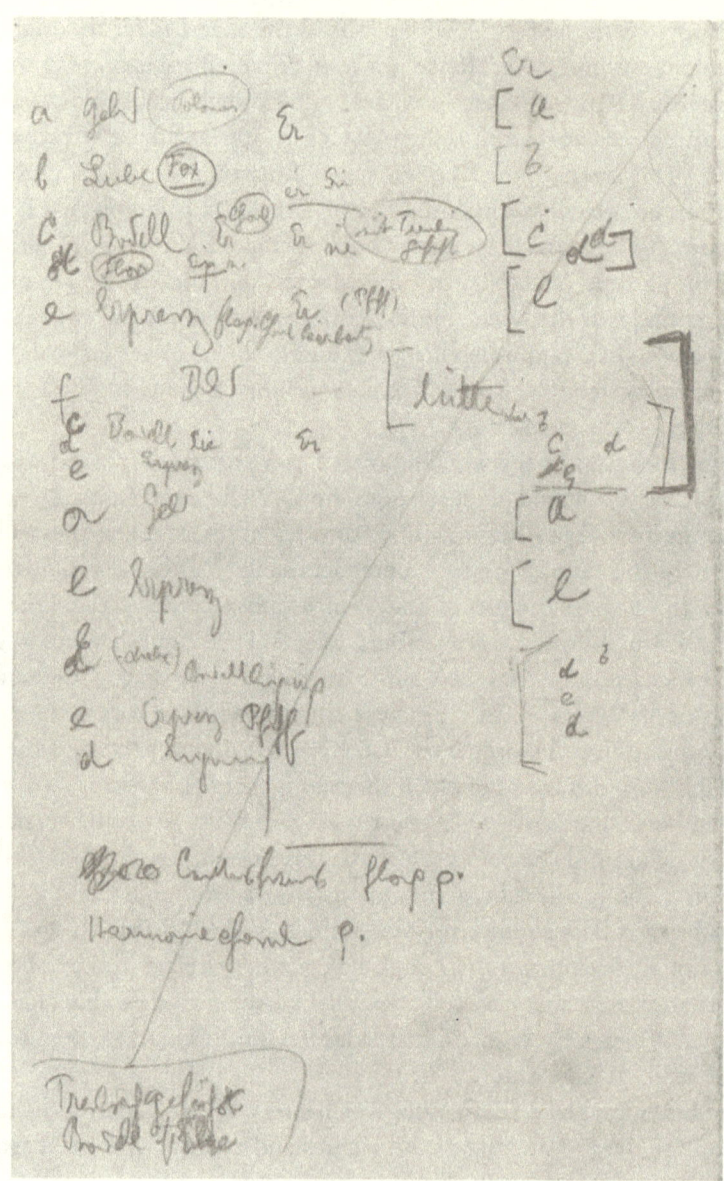

FIGURE 30. Form outline with "Treulich geführt" annotation. ÖNB Musiksammlung F 21 Berg 28/VI, fol. 6v

tion has begun; the revenge of the world of men which dares to avenge itself for its own guilt."[17] This line is from an introductory lecture on *Pandora's Box* that Kraus delivered for the play's debut in Vienna in 1905. Berg, even then an admirer of Wedekind, attended. Reich further comments on the occasion: "The impression made on Berg by Karl Kraus's production of *Pandora's Box* in Vienna was reinforced by Kraus's speech at the première, which he published shortly afterwards in his magazine, 'Die Fackel'. . . . Berg noted down parts of this speech at the time."[18] Reich goes on to quote sections from Karl Kraus's introduction, for as he explains, "Berg identified himself completely with the conception of the *Lulu* tragedy contained in Kraus' speech."[19] Berg's "complete identification" manifests itself not only in the double roles of the victims and clients but also in the theme of slavery and the association of the Prince and the Marquis, as shown by the following passage from Kraus's introductory lecture:

And then the powerful double tragedy, whose second part you'll watch today, the tragedy of the hunted, eternally misunderstood attraction of woman that a wretched world allows to fall into a Procrustean bed of moral beliefs. A gauntlet for woman, who was never intended by the will of God to serve the egotism of an owner, who can attain her higher worth only in freedom. No birdcatcher has ever said that the fleeting beauty of a tropical bird brings more joy than total ownership, even though the narrowness of the cage spoils the splendor of the plumage. The courtesan may well be man's dream. But the reality is that she becomes his slave—wife or mistress—because his need for social status exceeds his dream.[20]

Beyond these dramatic motivations, Berg had an equally important reason for equating the Prince and the Marquis relating to the opera's large-scale form. In a letter to Schoenberg, quoted at the opening of this chapter, Berg mentions that the singers who play the clients return in retrograde order in the last scene to project the opera's palindromic form. Further, in a letter to Reich, Berg discusses the quasi-symmetry of the two center scenes of *Lulu*, Act II, scene 1, and Act II, scene 2, for as Berg remarks, "The same characters take part in the dramatic action, both before and after the denouement."[21] The Prince and the Marquis appear in Act I, scene 3, and Act III, scene 1, which we see from Example 15 are also symmetrical scenes of the opera. By associating these two figures, through their similar music and the "Bordell ist Ehe" theme, Berg has devised yet another way to express the opera's palindromic form.

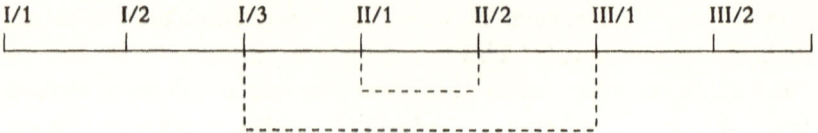

EXAMPLE 15. Scene symmetry of *Lulu*

The Manservant, the passive symbol of slavery, appears only in Act II, scene 1, the scene just preceding the center of the work. One would not expect, then, to see him as part of a neat symmetrical relation like that just noted between the Prince and the Marquis. However, Berg exploits the fact that Alwa employs Rodrigo the Acrobat in Act II, scene 2, as a servant, thereby concealing their plot to rescue Lulu from prison. And when Rodrigo makes his entrance in the middle of that scene in a servant's uniform to "serve" Alwa and Hugenberg, we hear the viola playing a grotesque imitation of the viola solo from the Manservant's music of Act II, scene 1 (Examples 16a and 16b). Dramatically, the music tells us that Rodrigo is now a distortion of the Manservant; formally, it tells us that we are now on the descending side of the opera, and that we are hearing another "darkened reminiscence" of an earlier event.[22]

Returning now to Figure 29, we see in the lower third of the sketch that Berg identifies the Theater Director, the Banker, and the Police Commissioner as "die Drei Schergen."[23] A "Scherge," according to the word's archaic definition, is the hangman's assistant—specifically, the one who finds the person to be hanged and delivers him up to the hangman for execution. Now, however, the word connotes a subservient official who somehow "does you in," and Berg uses this sense of the term in his sketch. The Theater Director, the "Scherge der Theater," acts as a sort of policeman for the theater. When Lulu abandons the stage in Act I, scene 3, because she sees Schön in the audience with his fiancée, the Theater Director immediately comes to Lulu's dressing room to return her to the stage. Kraus describes the Banker, the "Scherge des Finanz," as "demonically cunning"—one who "cheats society with his worthless stocks."[24] And finally, we have the Police Commissioner, the "Scherge der Polizei," who—like the archaic Scherge—comes to return Lulu to jail for the murder of Dr. Schön.[25]

In his book on *Lulu*, George Perle discusses the dramatic theme that unifies the double role of Rodrigo the Acrobat and the Animal Trainer who appears in the Prologue; Berg makes annotations in his sketches to the same effect. Perle notes that the general dramatic theme that connects the two roles is the circus.[26] Moreover, we again have the same quasi-symmetry of pairs in this group that we observed in the victims/clients and the slavery group. Rodrigo first appears in the Prologue as an animal trainer, and he introduces the various members of his menagerie, each of whom represents a character in the opera. Perle explains that when Rodrigo appears at the beginning of Act III, scene 1, and calls out to the society group, "Meine Herren und Damen," he is accompanied by the circus music of the Prologue, which is Berg's way of telling us that this highly decadent group of characters appearing in Act III, scene 1, is just another type of menagerie.[27]

When Rodrigo is not momentarily stepping out of his primary role to play the servant or the Animal Trainer, he is, of course, an acrobat. He has his own series, formed by extracting every second note from consecutive statements of the source row, and he appears in the music of the opera's center; Act II, scene 1, through Act III, scene 1.

Unfortunately, Berg left no sketches that show the general dramatic theme for the triple role of the Dresser, the Schoolboy, and Bob the Groom. Berg was undoubtedly aware of the convenience of using a single contralto to perform these roles, yet as with his other multiple roles, his intentions, I am convinced, went beyond this surface level. It is clear, for instance, that those in this group are among Lulu's saviors rather than her persecutors; the Dresser tries to convince the Theater Director not to return Lulu to the stage; the Schoolboy idolizes Lulu and in Act II, scene 2, devises a plan for her escape from prison. Bob, from Act III, scene 1, is instrumental in her escape from the Police Commissioner, for near the end of the scene he exchanges clothes with her and poses as Lulu when the Commissioner arrives.

One could further argue that this triple role is split into symmetrical pairs. The Schoolboy has his own twelve-tone row, formed by extracting every third note from successive statements of the source row. He appears in the two center scenes of the opera, first in Act II, scene 1, as an idolizing schoolboy who writes Lulu poetry and then again in Act II, scene 2, as an escapee from a reformatory who has a plan for Lulu's escape. The Dresser and Bob the Groom also appear in symmetrical scenes, Act I, scene 3, and Act III, scene 1. Both are subsidiary characters, with no separate twelve-tone row or specific thematic material. One wonders if

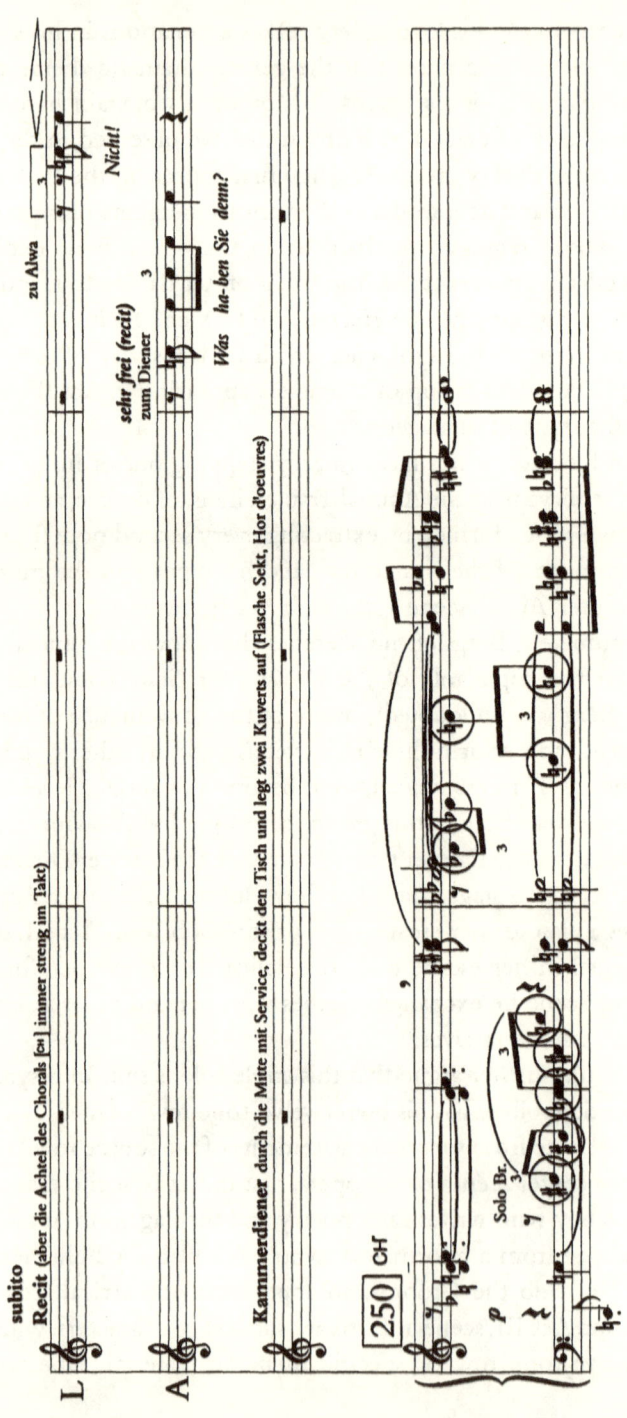

78 Interaction of Role and Form

EXAMPLES 16A (*facing page*) AND 16B (*above*). Manservant's music, Act II, scene 1, mm. 250–52, and Act II, scene 2, mm. 876–81

Interaction of Role and Form 79

Berg noted that each is a type of servant to Lulu or that each is involved in a "dressing motif." Without new information from Berg's sketches, however, we cannot know.

Berg did not always resort to grotesque parodies of characters from the first half of the opera to produce the feeling of descent that takes place in the second half. As we have seen with the Acrobat and the Schoolboy, Berg often places a character in a bizarre reworking of that same character's earlier dramatic situation; these reworkings are particularly concentrated in the center two scenes of the opera.[28] For instance, in Act II, scene 1, Alwa has a love scene with Lulu, who is then at the height of her beauty and wealth as the wife of Alwa's father, Dr. Schön. In Act II, scene 2, Alwa has a similar love scene with Lulu, now an emaciated cholera victim who has just escaped from prison. Alwa's first love scene ends with Lulu's saying, "I poisoned your mother," and the second with Lulu's question: "Isn't that the sofa that your father bled to death on?"

Lulu and Schigolch's two duets constitute another of these "déjà vu" pairings, one for which Berg left detailed and revealing sketches. The first takes place in Act I, scene 2, as Schigolch visits Lulu in her elegant apartment. The second is in Act III, scene 1, when he visits her again—now in her elegant Paris salon. Figure 31 and its transcription and translation, Examples 17a and 17b, show the extent to which the reminiscent quality of the two duets was planned. Berg's outline for Schigolch and Lulu's first duet in Act I, scene 2, appears on the right-hand side of Figure 31. The column of letters on the sketch represents the different musical passages Berg devised to accompany each text theme of their conversation. The left-hand outline in Figure 31 is for Schigolch and Lulu's duet in Act III, scene 1. Here Berg is searching for corresponding text themes for the two duets so that he can emphasize them with corresponding musical themes. Although the music of the duet's final version is not matched to the extent we see here, the segments of music that Berg did repeat are minutely planned.

Example 18a, for instance, is the section of music from Schigolch and Lulu's first duet (labeled A through I on Berg's outline). Schigolch and Lulu are sitting together, Schigolch touches Lulu's knee, and Lulu remarks, "And how long has it been since I danced?" The doorbell rings, and Lulu suddenly draws herself away from Schigolch to answer it. The corresponding segment of music from Lulu and Schigolch's second duet (appearing in Example 18b) begins with Schigolch's asking, "And how long has it been since we were together?" He pulls Lulu toward him, and just as Lulu breaks away, we hear the ghost of the doorbell from their previous duet.

Example 19a shows the first half of another repeated segment, the section from the first duet where Schigolch swears he would do anything for Lulu. This music appears again in the second duet (Example 19b), when he again swears his dedication to Lulu, but now because he promises to murder her blackmailer, Rodrigo.

If we consider the total effect of a musical and dramatic reprise of this type—whether the same character appears in two analogous dramatic situations or the same singer in multiple roles—we see Berg's early conception of the opera's palindromic form that he expressed in his sketches become progressively more concrete. If we graph out Berg's various pairings of characters in his opera (as they appear in Example 20), we see how, working within the confines of the Wedekind text, Berg was able to achieve this symmetry. The technique of equating two different characters, in fact, recalls Berg's scenario for the Film Music for *Lulu*—a miniature and literal palindrome—where he pairs not only characters but also analogous objects and scenes for the same effect.[29] For instance, Lulu's trial in the first half of the scenario is matched with her consultation in the hospital in the second half; the judge and jury at the trial are matched with the doctors and students in the second half; and her resignation is matched with her awakening to live.

While the symbolism behind Berg's role doublings is admittedly hidden, that should not diminish the importance of the doublings themselves, for they influence the opera at every level. Like Kraus's introductory lecture on *Pandora's Box,* they bring out Wedekind's hidden themes, they unify diverse characters into distinct groups; they even accentuate the opera's slightly surreal quality. Most important, however, is their overall dramatic effect. For with *Lulu,* the "revenge of the world of men," like the shadowing of earlier events, begins not with the last scene, but with the opening of the last half of the opera.[30] And it is Berg's ingenious use of multiple roles that lets it take place.

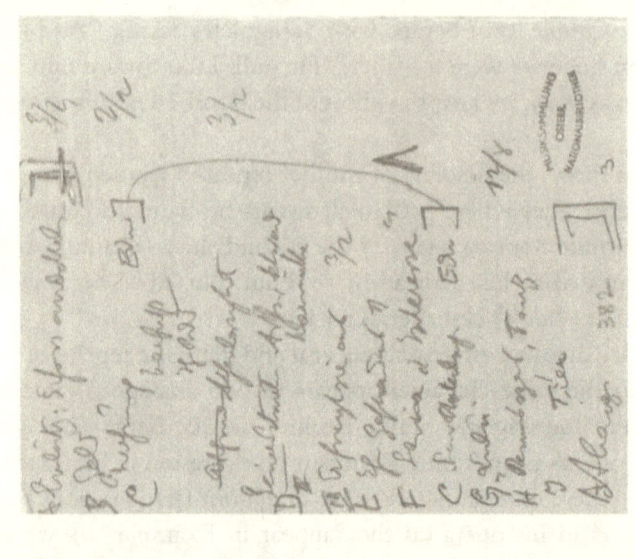
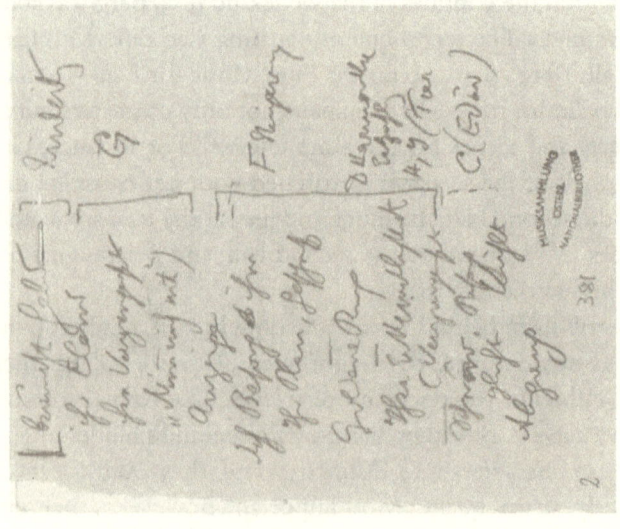

FIGURE 31. Form outline for the duets between Lulu and Schigolch in Act I, scene 2, and Act III, scene 1. ÖNB Musiksammlung F 21 Berg 28/XLVI, fols. 2r and 3r

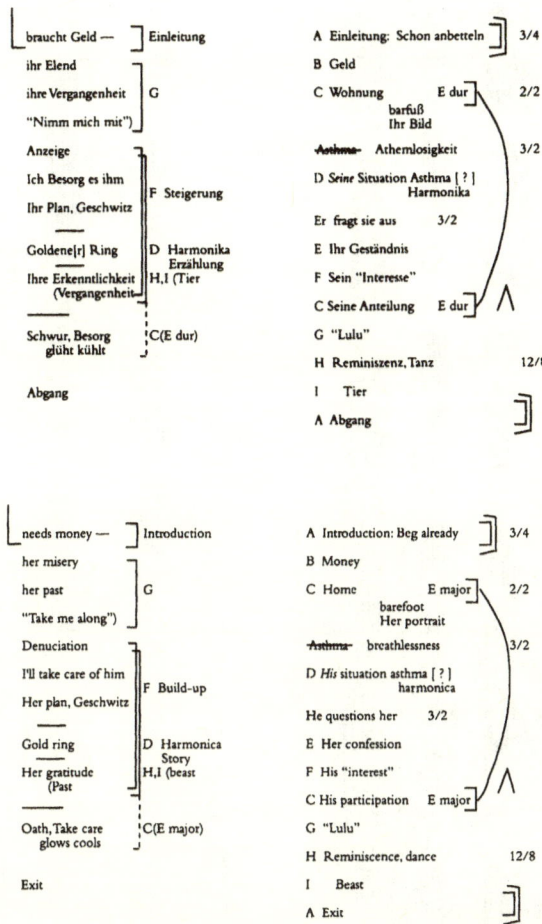

EXAMPLES 17A AND 17B. Transcription and translation of F 21 Berg 28/XLVI, fols. 2r and 3r

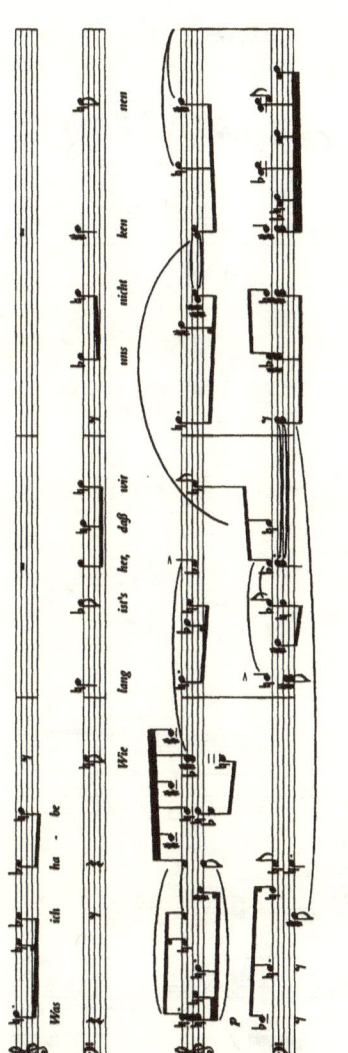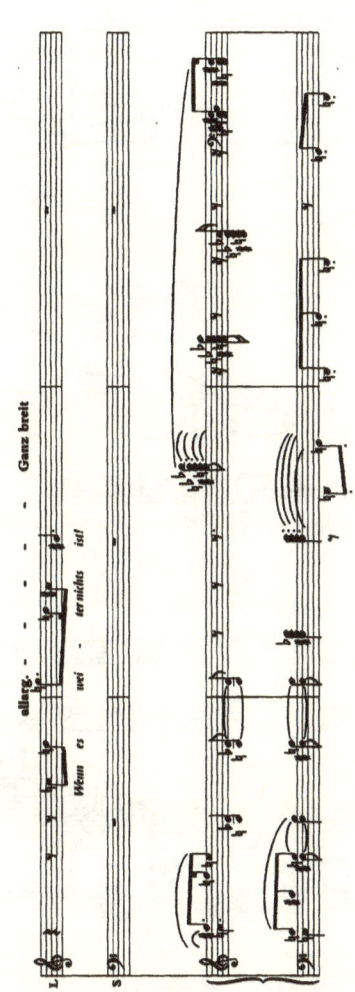

EXAMPLES 18A AND 18B. Duet between Lulu and Schigolch, Act I, scene 2, mm. 517–21, and Act III, scene 1, mm. 441–46

Interaction of Role and Form 85

EXAMPLE 19A. Duet between Lulu and Schigolch, Act I, scene 3, mm. 507–13

EXAMPLE 19B. Duet between Lulu and Schigolch, Act III, scene 1, mm. 445–60

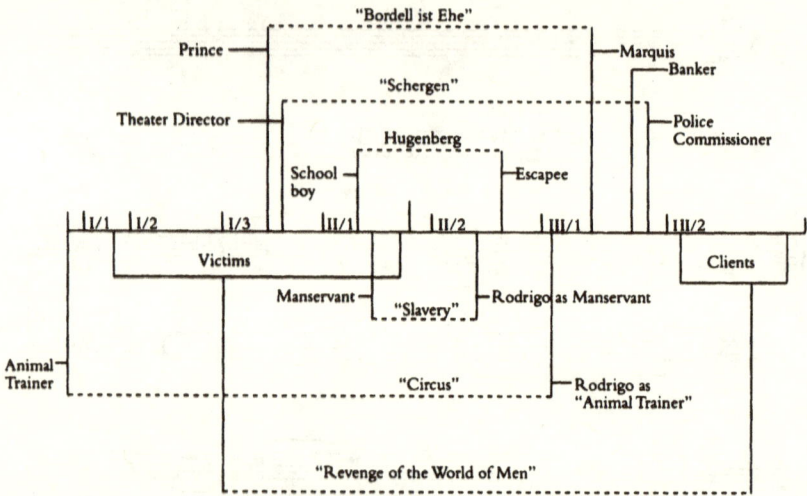

EXAMPLE 20. Summary of multiple roles

Chapter 4

Derivational Unfoldings
The Case of Dr. Schön

While Chapter 3 solved an enigma relating to the opera's overall form, Chapter 4 focuses on a smaller level of structure, the Sonata that dominates the opera's first act. I have chosen it because Berg's sketches for it elaborate features of his compositional process set forth in Chapter 1 and clarify the function of three controversial passages. I begin by investigating the origins of the controversy in the writings of Reich and Perle.

Near the end of Act II, scene 1, of *Lulu,* as Dr. Schön, murdered by Lulu, lies dying, a musical event as unusual as the dramatic one that inspires it takes place: the notes of Dr. Schön's row gradually subside back into the source row from which they were derived. While this musical event has an obvious symbolic meaning, what Carner calls "the ebbing away of his life as the third and most important of Lulu's victims," it also has a clear theoretical one: it demonstrates musically the relation between one of the opera's subsidiary rows and its source row.[1] This relation figures as the key issue in an ongoing controversy that surrounds the work. The controversy originated in an article on *Lulu* written shortly after Berg's death by his student Willi Reich, in which Reich, basing his assertion on Berg's own words, states that "the strictest musical cohesion is achieved in *Lulu* by deriving the entire musical action of the opera from a single twelve-tone row."[2] Reich then outlines the operations Berg used to derive the

EXAMPLE 21. Derivation of Dr. Schön's row from the source row

subsidiary rows of the opera from the source row. Berg forms Dr. Schön's row, for instance, by omitting notes in a palindromic pattern from three consecutive statements of the source row (Example 21). He first omits one note, then two, then three, then the reverse—three notes, two, and one—until only the twelve notes of Dr. Schön's row remain.

Reich's musical proof of his one-row hypothesis—and in particular how it effected the unity of the opera—hardly went beyond these row derivations, however; and in 1959 Perle challenged Reich, saying that his interpretation had little relevance to the actual music of the opera: "Reich's so-called analysis is mainly a description by means of which Berg ostensibly generated these auxiliary sets from the basic set. It could not possibly have been derived from the only valid source, the composition, which doesn't present a shred of evidence to support his description."[3]

Specifically, Perle contends that most of Reich's derivative operations are precompositional procedures, for the literal derivation of the subsidiary row from the source row—that is, its derivational unfolding—does not specifically occur in the music itself. Consequently, the relationship between the source row and its derivation shown in Reich's analysis is never established, and the listener hears the many different subsidiary rows of the opera as independent of the source row.[4]

Perle's rebuttal of Reich's analysis spurred a new stage in the debate: musicologists searched the passages of *Lulu* to see if more unfoldings really did exist. As it now stands, Reich's one-row hypothesis has not been substantiated, for no one has been able to dispute that very few of the subsidiary rows are related to the source row via unfoldings. But while the absence of these unfoldings seems to solve the one-row controversy, it leaves us with many questions about the function of the unfoldings themselves. For if Berg's purpose in writing them was primarily to demonstrate the relation between a subsidiary row and the source row, why did he do so for a few of the rows, but not for the rest?

Moreover, two of the three unfoldings associated with the character Dr. Schön either are so incomplete or contain so many extraneous notes that their derivational function seems, if anything, contradicted. It is in our attempt to answer these kinds of questions that Berg's sketches prove helpful.

Until now, the only sketches cited with reference to this issue are the few that Reich later published in defense of his own analysis.[5] These sketches do indeed document Berg's methods of deriving his subsidiary rows, but unfortunately they tell us nothing more than Reich's original article about the passages in question.

The sketches that became accessible in 1981, in contrast, show the actual details of the passages and reveal other programmatic and theoretical insights that are not readily apparent from the finished work. The purpose of this chapter, then, is to show through selected form, row, and compositional sketches that these unfoldings are not simply derivational; they also express dramatic symbolism as a large-scale event. Specifically, I document and expand an idea first put forth by Klaus Schweizer about a leitmotivic use of these derivational passages.[6] I further argue that only a few characters have unfoldings because the function of these characters in the plot made this technique appropriate only for them. This chapter centers on one of these characters, Dr. Schön, and I examine sketches I have found to illustrate how Berg varies unfoldings to mirror the dramatic situation, often to the point that their derivational property is minimized. Since two of these passages occur in themes from the Sonata of Act I and derive their dramatic meaning from its plot, I must begin with an overview of this music and its relation to the text.

The Sonata of Act I represents the character Dr. Schön. Specifically, it is the epic of his struggle to finally break his ties with Lulu by marrying the woman to whom he has been engaged for three years. Berg constructs the Sonata in two halves that arise out of two different dialogues between Schön and Lulu in the Wedekind text. In the first half, which makes up the exposition and first reprise in Act I, scene 2, Schön visits Lulu shortly after her husband, the Painter, has left to work in his adjoining studio. Schön will be married soon, and he demands of Lulu that their secret affair come to an end. Lulu, however, cannot bear to set Schön free, and the noise of their ensuing argument eventually causes Lulu's husband to return to find out what is wrong. With the Painter's entrance, the Sonata breaks off until the middle of the next scene, which presents the development and second reprise.

Like the exposition, the development begins during another of Schön's agitated visits to Lulu; however, this time the setting is her theater dressing room. Lulu, who is starring as a dancer in a work composed by Schön's son, Alwa, has seen Schön in the audience with his fiancée and now refuses to dance. During the resulting argument over his approaching marriage, Schön realizes that he is powerless to end his relationship with Lulu—a realization signaled in the music by the beginning of the second reprise. Lulu dictates the letter to Schön in which he admits this attachment to his fiancée and ends his engagement. The Sonata ends with the coda theme and Schön's prophetic words: "Now comes the execution."

While most of the text for the Sonata centers on the relationship between Schön and Lulu, two other characters, Schön's fiancée and Lulu's husband, also figure prominently, and scholars have often noted that Berg seems to pair each of the four sections of the exposition with a passage in the text depicting one of these four characters.[7] Berg's sketches support this idea, as well as revealing additional important details. Figure 32, for instance, shows Berg's sketch for the form of the Sonata, with its transcription and translation appearing as Examples 22a and 22b. As we can see, Berg has arranged the titles of the four sections of the Sonata in columns with the text theme appearing directly beneath. The principal theme of the Sonata (column 1) represents Schön (in Berg's words), "the complete personality, multi-sided, domineering, possessed by deep feeling." The bridge passage depicts not only Lulu's husband, Walter, but the other men in her life. The subordinate theme (column 3) is for Schön's fiancée, "the bride." And finally, Berg entitles the coda "the possession," referring to the relationship between Lulu and Dr. Schön.

What is most remarkable about the Sonata is that each time the exposition returns as a reprise, Berg retains this pairing of character and sonata theme. Thus, if we look at column three, "the bride," we see that the first time the subordinate theme appears, Lulu is praising Schön's fiancée: "She's blossomed into a charming young girl." When the subordinate theme returns in the first reprise, however, Schön and Lulu are arguing over his bride: "You think I'm jealous of that child?" asks Lulu. "I never

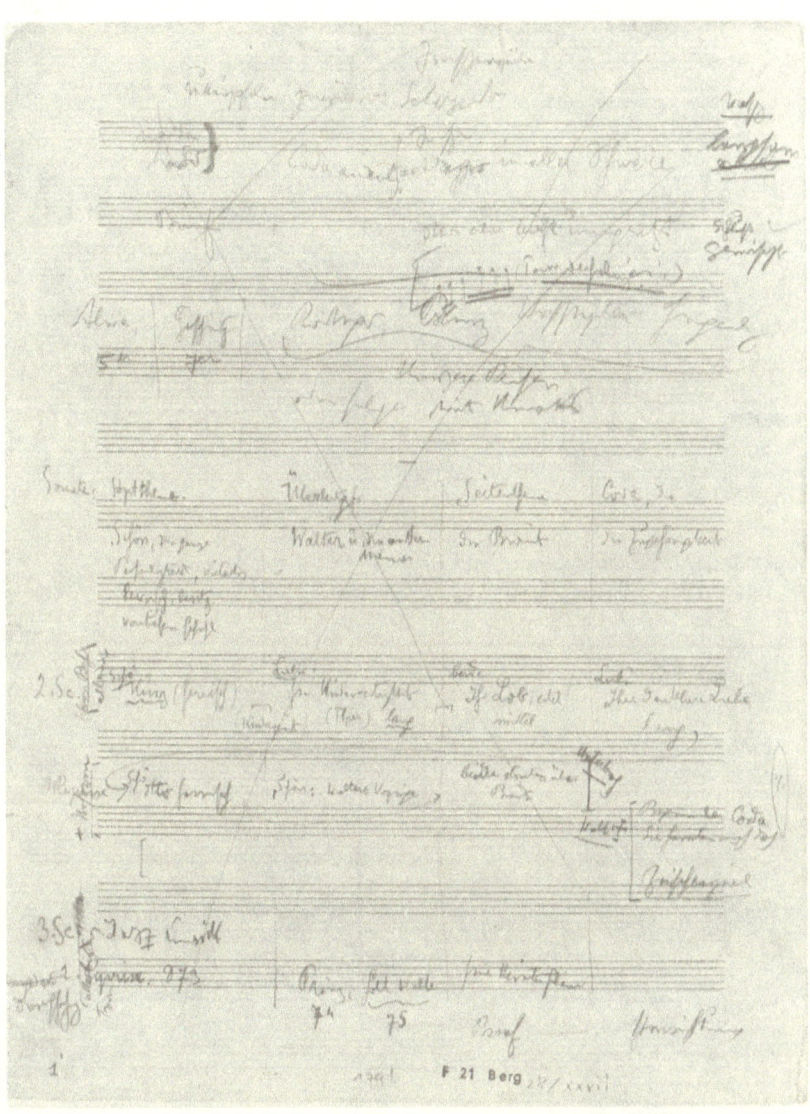

FIGURE 32. Form sketch of the Sonata. ÖNB Musiksammlung F 21 Berg 28/XXVII, fol. 1v

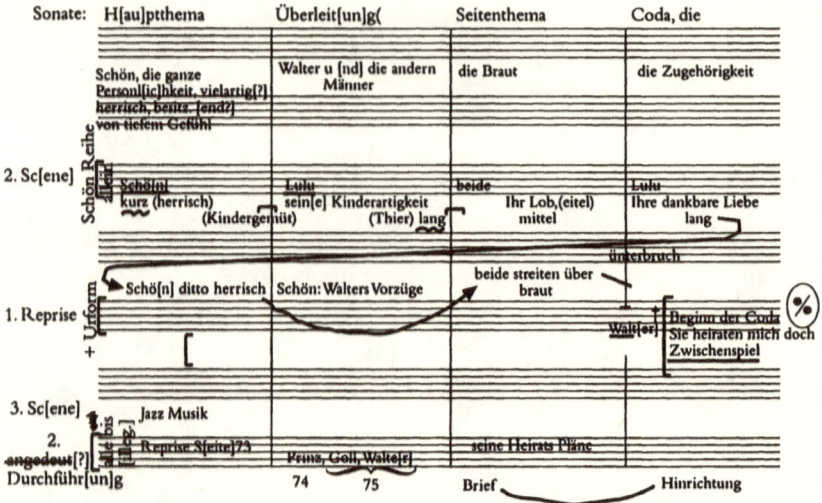

EXAMPLE 22A. Transcription of F 21 Berg 28/XXVII, fol. 1v, staves 6–12 (see Figure 32)

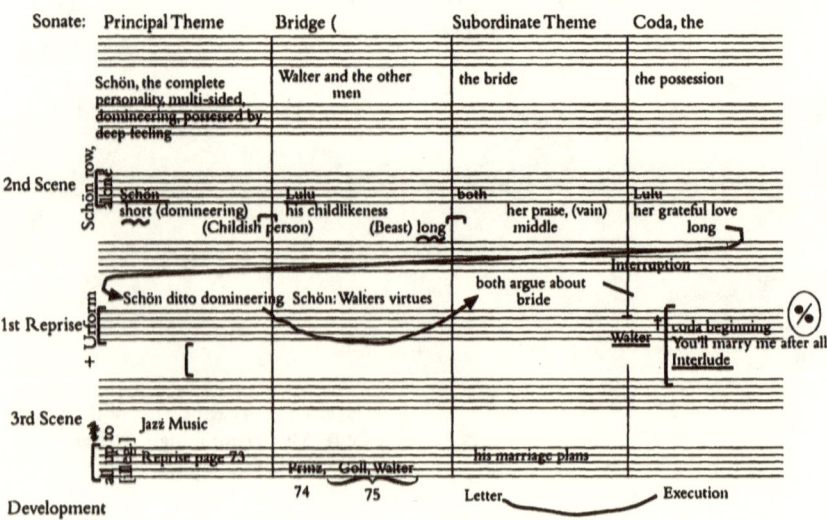

EXAMPLE 22B. Translation of F 21 Berg 28/XXVII, fol. 1v, staves 6–12 (see Figure 32)

noticed that!" Schön responds: "Why do you call her a child? She's only a year younger than you." The final time the subordinate theme appears, Schön has realized that he can no longer return to his fiancée; it is here that Lulu dictates "the letter" in which he ends his engagement.

By using this parallel construction between text and musical theme, Berg in a sense strengthens the given structure of the Sonata—a goal he vividly expressed in a letter to Webern written July 23, 1931: "Now the difficulty is (one of the thousand difficulties); to work the music, which is conditioned by musical laws, into the Wedekind text, which is determined by dialectical laws, make the two coincide and span over it the powerful arc of the action."[8]

As a structuring device Berg uses not only text but also the tempi of the exposition themes, for he pairs each of them with a specific metronome marking. In some of his earliest sketches for the Sonata Berg assigns to the principal theme the tempo of 80 1/2 beats per minute (later rounded off to 80); to the bridge passage, 46; to the secondary theme, 69; and to the coda, 57 1/2 (later rounded off to 58).[9] One of Berg's notes in the *Particell* to *Lulu* clarifies the significance of these numbers: they are all based on Berg's own number, 23. Berg tells us: "N.B. 23/2 = 11 1/2. 11 1/2 × 4 = 46 (the tempo of the bridge passage). 11 1/2 × 5 = 57 1/2 (the tempo of the coda); and 11 1/2 × 6 and 7 gives 69 and 80 1/2 (the tempi of the second subject and the first subject)."[10]

Like Berg's tempo manipulations, the first of Dr. Schön's derivational unfoldings is written cryptically. It occurs in the opening of the main theme of the Sonata. (In the drama, this is where Schön, entering Lulu's apartment, notices Schigolch, her alleged father, slipping out and remarks: "If I were your husband, this person wouldn't come over the threshold.") The function of this passage has generated a great deal of controversy. In the discussion that follows I examine the various views and then see what new insights Berg's sketches provide.

Klaus Schweizer, the first of three musicologists to describe this passage as a "compositional working out" of the derivation of Schön's row, analyzes the passage in the manner shown in Example 23a (summarized in Example 23b).[11] If we compare the summary of the unfolding to Schweizer's analysis of it, we see that the passage—like Schön's row derivation—consists of three complete statements of the source row. If we think of the unfolding as having two components, that is, the notes of

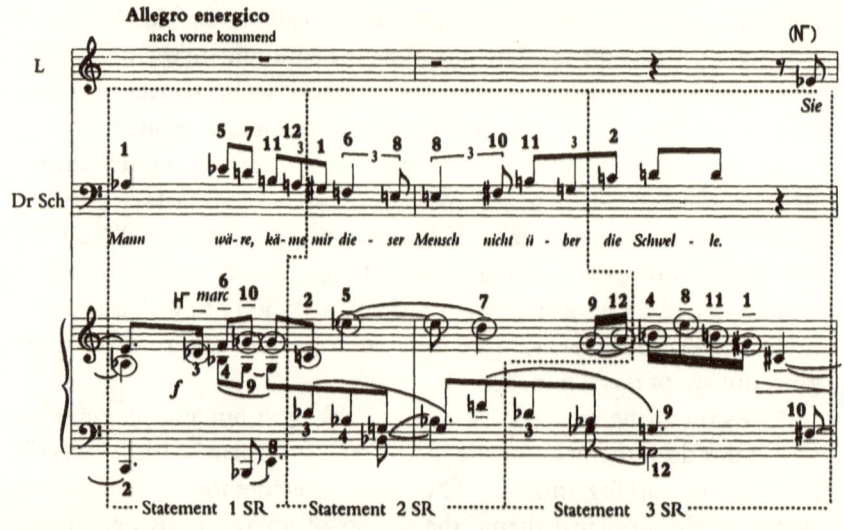

EXAMPLES 23A AND 23B. Schweizer's analysis of the unfolding in the main theme of the Sonata, Act I, scene 2, mm. 533–34, and summary graph

Dr. Schön's row and the remaining notes of the source row, then these two layers are here completely separate. Dr. Schön's row is self-contained in his "man of power" theme (appearing on staff three) and the remaining notes of the source row are distributed between the vocal line and the accompaniment.

An important discrepancy between this unfolding and Berg's derivation, however, is that approximately half the notes of the source row do not occur in their proper sequence between the notes of Schön's row. Furthermore, there are many extraneous notes, such as the B flat and D flat (third staff, m. 1), that seem to have nothing to do with the unfolding. These discrepancies, along with the general inaudibility of the relation of Schön's row to the source row, have caused Perle and Jarman to discount this passage as evidence for the one-row controversy, for as Perle notes, "[The unfolding] does not project the derivational procedure at all and is not in principle to be distinguished from countless other passages in which notes common to both sets simultaneously function as members of both."[12] Further, Jarman remarks:

> Such a practice is not uncommon in Berg's twelve-note music but seems inadmissible in a passage, the supposed function of which is to demonstrate the derivation from the basic series of one of the most important sets of the work. Indeed, such omissions and alterations would appear to invalidate the whole procedure.[13]

But what do Berg's sketches tell us?

Figure 33a (transcribed in Example 24a) shows an early sketch of the opening of the main theme of the Sonata in which Berg uses the graphic notation described in Chapter 1. As I remarked there, Berg typically uses this notation to indicate the durations of the notes, but not their exact pitches. He used it as a shorthand for passages whose notes he already knew (we can see, for instance, the contour of Schön's theme on staff 2), or he used it as a method for mapping out the syllabic stress of the vocal line before he added pitches to it. Staff 1 of the sketch shows this later technique.

Figure 33b and its transcription in Example 24b show a slightly later sketch of the same passage, with pitches assigned to the earlier graphic notes. Beneath the pitches one can see the rhythmic skeleton of the vocal line; the opening of the main theme, representing Schön, is also present, but transposed to P_8. In this sketch, unlike the earlier one, Berg writes between the notes of Dr. Schön's row each of the omitted notes of the source row in their correct order. As one might suspect from the finished score, it was after setting up the vocal line and Dr. Schön's theme that Berg added the remaining notes of the source row. And one can see where he has begun to cross them off methodically as he fits them here and there into the accompaniment.

Annotations such as these leave little doubt that the passage is a compositional working out of the derivation of Schön's row from the source row—a fact we might easily overlook in the finished score. Thus, Perle's statement that "[the unfolding] is not in principle to be distinguished from countless other passages in which notes common to both sets simultaneously function as members of both" is incorrect. At the same time, however, one must agree that the overriding function of this par-

FIGURES 33a and 33b. Sketches for the unfolding in the main theme of the Sonata. ÖNB Musiksammlung F 21 Berg 28/XXVI, fols. 8r and 14r, staves 1–4.

EXAMPLES 24A AND 24B. Transcriptions of F 21 Berg 28/XXVI, fols. 8r and 14r, staves 1–4

ticular unfolding is not to demonstrate the relation of Schön's row to the source row, for Berg has expressed this relation in far too hidden (or, if you will, sophisticated) a manner. As becomes clear from later sketches, this passage—like the unfolding in Schön's death scene—functions as a metaphor for Schön's eventual death at Lulu's hand. Since this does not occur until Act II, scene 1, a "bona fide" and complete unfolding cannot take place until that moment without contradicting the drama. Schweizer understands this function in that he describes the two unfold-

EXAMPLE 25. "Fate rhythm" in the theme of the coda

ings as a continuum. At Schön's death, he explains, the notes of his row merge with the remaining notes of the source row and become indistinguishable; at the beginning of the conflict then, we have the opposite situation: the independence of Schön's row seems to leave the remaining notes of the source row behind.[14]

Sketches are useful in clarifying the intention of the composer in this passage of the Sonata. While theorists have certainly been aware of the passage itself, Berg's careful annotations reveal its actual function. In the next unfolding of Schön's music, sketches bring to our attention a similar event, which scholars have, ironically, hardly mentioned. It takes place in the coda of the Sonata.

The music of the coda has always been a favorite of *Lulu* scholars. Hans Redlich describes its theme as "one of Berg's most deeply felt melodic inspirations," and Perle calls it "the most memorable melodic element of the opera."[15] The coda's expressive effect derives, in part, from its dramatic meaning, for it is here that Lulu, reacting to Schön's wish to be free of her, professes her love to him. Lulu's attachment to Schön will soon result in his death, however, and Berg suggests this by setting the melody of the coda to durations of the fate rhythm (Example 25). Variations of this rhythm accompany the deaths of many of the opera's characters.

In Chapter 1, I noted that Berg rarely made successive revisions; rather, he moved immediately from one stage of sketch to the next. In contrast to that practice, Berg sketched the coda repeatedly, making only slight changes each time. The earliest and most revealing of these sketches dates from the fall of 1929, when, as I determined in Chapter 2, Berg first developed Dr. Schön's row.[16] The sketch appears as Figure 34; two sections of it are transcribed in Examples 26a and 26b. The first of these transcriptions, consisting of the first staff of Berg's sketch, shows the

FIGURE 34. Sketch of the derivation of Schön's row from the source row (staff 1) and early sketch of the coda (staves 7–17). ÖNB Musiksammlung F 21 Berg 28/X, fol. 1r

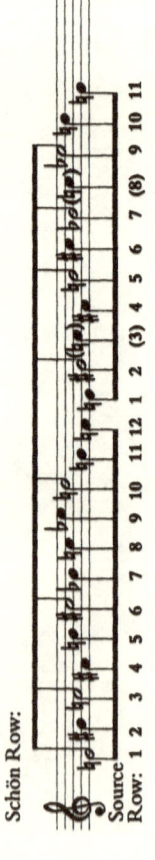

EXAMPLES 26A, 26B, AND 26C. Transcriptions of F 21 Berg 28/X, fol. 1r, staves 1 and 7–8 (see Figure 34), and summary graph of the unfolding in the coda

Derivational Unfoldings: Dr. Schön

process by which Berg derived Dr. Schön's row from the source row. Berg writes out the three necessary statements of the source row, marking those notes that will form Dr. Schön's row with upward stems, or naming them in small circles between the notes of Schön's row.

On staves 7–9 of Berg's sketch appears one of Berg's earliest drafts of the coda, written without the "fate rhythm" of the final version. To the left of the sketch Berg writes: "mit Entstehung aus [der] Urreihe" (with genesis from the source row). If we look at the sketch carefully, we can see that Berg has actually worked out two different solutions for an unfolding; the first of these is transcribed in Example 26b and summarized in Example 26c.

Berg wrote the unfolding for the coda, unlike that in the opening of the main theme, using its two components from the very beginning. This unfolding consists of two, rather than three, complete statements of the source row, labeled only with the order numbers of that source row. Schön's row predominates slightly, for Berg has placed the notes of his row into the melodic line (written with upward stems) and the remaining notes of the source row in their proper sequence into the accompaniment (written with downward stems).

Berg's title for the coda, "the possession," as well as the words the unfolding sets forth make the unusual dramatic symbolism clear. For the two rows begin to unfold as Lulu says to Schön, "If I belong to anyone in this world I belong to you," and Schön's row literally belongs to Lulu's row, the source row of the opera.[17] Example 27 displays this passage as it appears in its final version. Berg has now set the melodic line to durations of the fate rhythm; this admittedly makes the unfolding less clear, but as with the main theme, it is the hidden metaphor and large-scale context—not just the row derivation—that govern this passage. Another unfolding begins near the middle of the coda (m. 622), where Lulu, recounting how Schön has helped her in the past, cries, "Do you think I could forget that?" But now, as in the drama, Schön draws away from Lulu, and the connection between Schön's row and the source row becomes progressively more abstract, until, with his "Let me out of this!" the unfolding breaks off completely and Schön's "man of power" theme begins the reprise of the Sonata.

The last and most extended of Dr. Schön's derivational unfoldings takes place at his death in Act II, scene 1, where, despite his efforts to free

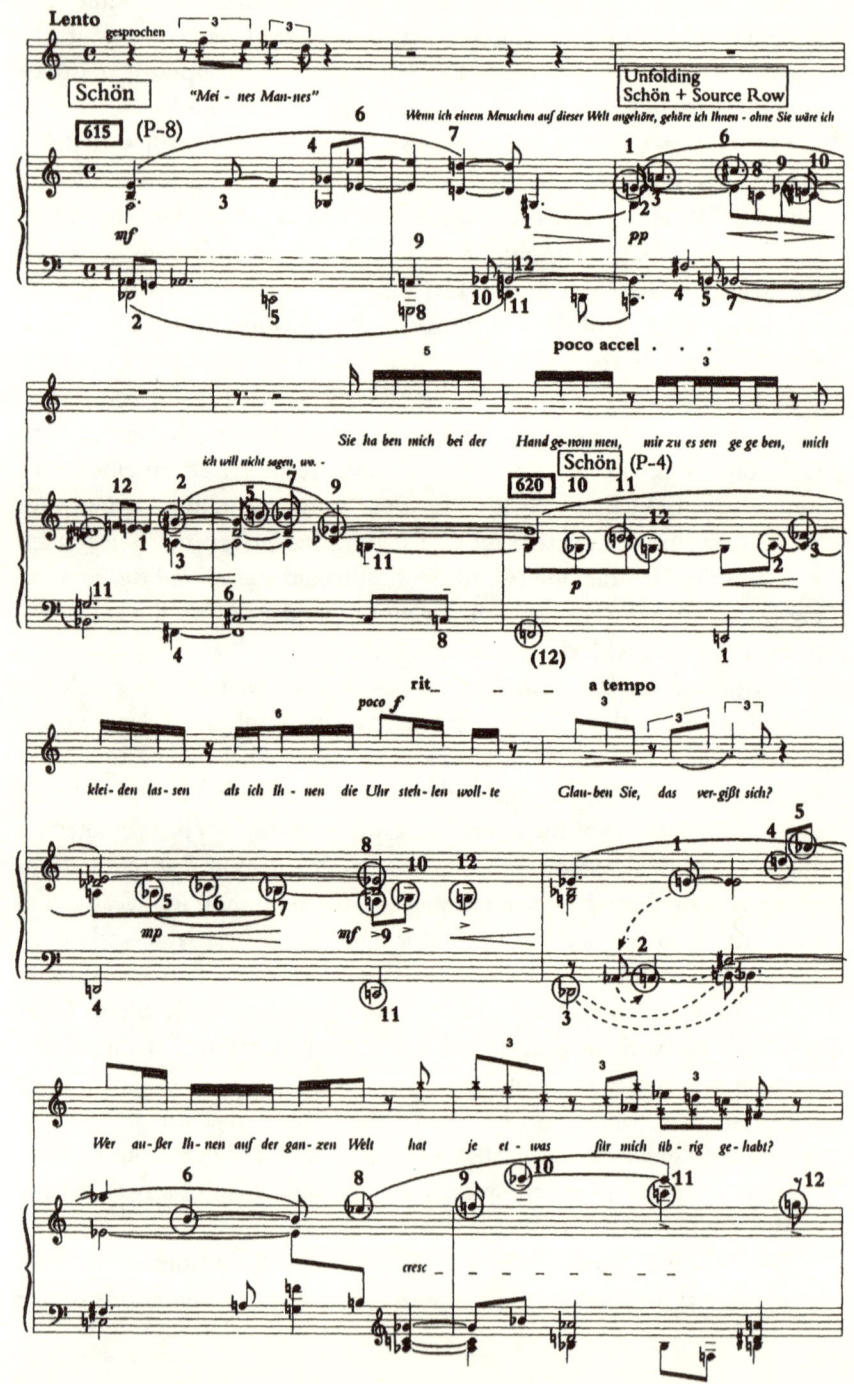

EXAMPLE 27. Coda, Act I, scene 2, mm. 615–24, and opening of the reprise of the Sonata

himself of Lulu, Schön has now become the third of her unhappy husbands. After the shock of secretly observing his son, Alwa, in her arms, Schön makes one final attempt to be rid of her: he gives Lulu a revolver and commands her to shoot herself. In a moment of distraction, however, Lulu turns the gun on Schön instead, and as Schön lies dying, the unfolding begins. This extended passage takes place in three parts, which are summarized in the music of Example 28.

The first part (mm. 587–90) sets forth a simple statement of Schön's row at P_4, the same transposition level as the unfolding in the coda. The second part follows in mm. 591–602, after Berg's stage cue "Schön drinks with a last glance at Lulu and her portrait." It is a statement of Schön's row (again at P_4); however, now the "missing notes" from the source row are also present until the third part, mm. 603–4. With Schön's cries of "Oh God, Oh God," nothing remains but the victorious source row representing Lulu.

Many musicologists have noted the obvious dramatic symbolism behind this event—symbolism verified in Berg's sketches. In one of them, for the form of Act II, scene 1, Berg writes: "Schön's death, retrograde evolution of Schön's row to the Lulu row."[18] As we have seen from Berg's sketches, the unfolding of Schön's death scene is also part of what one could call a large-scale retrograde evolution. Schön's row is generated from the source row as he steps onstage at the beginning of the Sonata; the rows appear intertwined in the coda as Lulu desperately expresses her love for him; and finally his row is absorbed at his death into the source row. These three types of unfolding are summarized in the three stages of Schön's death scene: Schön's row alone (stage 1), followed by the two rows intertwined (stage 2), followed by the source row alone (stage 3). It should not be surprising that Berg constructed this dramatic event over such a large span. It recalls, in fact, his use of multiple roles, discussed in Chapter 3, where widely spaced repetitions of musical passages helped unify the entire opera.

That Berg used this leitmotivic technique for Schön, the central figure in Lulu's life and the most resistant of her victims, also seems fitting. There are frequent references in the text that might have given Berg the idea, such as Lulu's comment in the development "You're too weak to rip yourself away from me!" or Schön's recurring plea "Do let me free!"

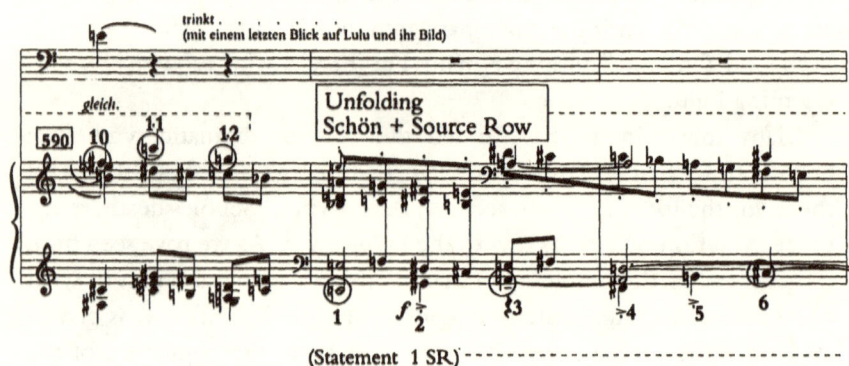

EXAMPLE 28. The unfolding in Dr. Schön's death scene, Act II, scene 1, mm. 587–604

Derivational Unfoldings: Dr. Schön

With the Manservant, however, one of the other characters given a lengthy derivational passage, the unfolding represents, not this fateful pulling toward death, but rather dependency. The Manservant's row is derived by extracting notes from successive statements of Alwa's row, the source row (representing Lulu), and Dr. Schön's row. At the top of the sketch for the Manservant's unfolding Berg reminds us that he is "dependent on Alwa, Lulu, and Schön."[19]

Berg's unfoldings, as revealed by his sketches, show a mastery of dramatic symbolism, as well as an effective means of unifying Schön's music. Still, this leaves us with an apparent contradiction, a lack of evidence to support Berg's claim that the music of *Lulu* is unified through his use of a single twelve-tone row. I return to this problem in Chapter 5, where through selected correspondence and sketches, I show that Berg based his comment primarily on inherent properties of the rows rather than his presentation of these rows in the opera. To understand the true meaning of Berg's unfoldings, we might well refer to his heartfelt comment about *Wozzeck,* for it applies equally well to *Lulu:*

I had nothing else in mind at the moment when I decided to write an opera, nothing else in mind even as regards the technique of composition, than to render to the theatre what is the theatre's, and that means to shape the music in such a way that it is aware in every moment of its duty to serve the drama.[20]

Chapter 5

The Progress of a Method

Berg's Tone Rows for *Lulu*

In a letter to Webern written September 20, 1929, Berg confides:

My present work is not progressing well at all. There are days when I don't feel up to the task. Probably also with regard to "row" composition. But I believe that I have now found a solution to the *problem* of making o n e row suffice for a work lasting several hours. (Apart from the various forms that I had already derived for it long ago.)
You'll see what I have discovered from the enclosed sheet of staff paper. Of course from the mathematical point of view it is obvious. But in the musical practice of row composition, it is something that perhaps no one has yet discovered, something that—as I've said—can be applied to every twelve-tone row.[1]

Although Berg's letter survives, the "enclosed sheet of staff paper" that he mentions has been lost, and consequently the exact nature of his discovery remains unclear. An added mystery, as Douglas Jarman has noted, is that Berg had already written Schoenberg the previous year about the kind of row derivation he uses in *Lulu*, the "work lasting several hours" to which he refers.[2] Moreover, we know that by 1929 Berg was well into the composition of *Lulu*—past the time when one would expect him to be deriving new twelve-tone rows.[3]

Fortunately, however, Berg also corresponded with his student Willi Reich about his discovery. And Reich's responses, coupled with Berg's sketches, not only reveal its nature, but also give us new insight into Berg's claim that the music of *Lulu* is based on a single twelve-tone row.

The fall of 1929 was a time of discovery for both Berg and Reich. The latter writes in his biography of the composer that he visited Berg in Trahütten on August 23, the day Berg finished the fair copy of his soprano aria *Der Wein*.[4] Apparently their discussion brought Reich new ideas, which he later detailed in correspondence, for he informs us that as a result of his visit "I also wrote [to Berg] about 'complementary series' in which it was possible—on account of their special construction— knowing a few of the notes, to deduce the rest."[5]

In his letters to Berg, Reich defines a complementary series as a row whose inversion is identical to its retrograde; this property results from a mirror relation between the two principal hexachords of the row. Reich's letters are filled with excitement about the properties he is discovering in complementary rows. The most important of these, he believes, is that the entire series can be derived from only its first six pitches. Reich refers to these pitches as the "determining tones" of the series and notes that if one presents only five or four of these determining tones, the rows they imply become progressively more ambiguous. One could use this property, Reich states, to create a sort of pivot area "which makes modulation between closely related twelve-tone rows possible."[6]

In late September Berg began corresponding with Reich about his own discovery; the only information we have about these letters, however, is what Reich provides in his biography of Berg:

Shortly afterwards (20th and 21st September) he gave me exhaustive information about two sorts of complementary series which one could make use of "if, in a work of several hours like an opera, one believes that a single series is not sufficient, or at least for the sake of a change." This remark refers directly to his work on the opera *Lulu* in which he uses such series to a considerable extent.[7]

Reich's responses to Berg's two letters are dated September 21 and 25. In the first of these he writes:

Your information about row transformation is fabulously interesting and affects me particularly because it runs along the same lines as my own research and even anticipates my shorthand, which, like yours, is completely independent of transposition. Apparently other, actually higher, connections do exist here. The reason that *only* the fifth, seventh, and eleventh pitches work seems to be that $1 + 11$ and $5 + 7$ are the only pure prime numbers of 12; moreover, $5 + 7 + 11 = 23$.[8]

The nature of Berg's "row transformation" is not explicitly clear from this letter; however, in his second letter Reich offers more details:

Thank you very much for your dear postcard, which provided me the longed-for completion of your newly developed discovery of the Bergian rows B_5 and B_7—namely the musical interpretation, since after all the mathematical is only of secondary importance to a musician, interesting as it too might be per se. It's also rather curious how the whole thing shapes up when you use as the original row a row of the complementary type that I established. Then the inversions play all manner of roles and the circle closes as early as the first degree relationship. I've worked out some things on the enclosed sheet of staff paper, but it's possible to show still more.

A universal property of *every* B_5 and B_7 is the following: in the former every third, in the latter every second tone is identical to the original row.[9]

Reich's letters supply us with nearly enough information to decipher Berg's discovery. His terms B_5 and B_7, for instance, call to mind the rows Berg uses in *Lulu* for the characters Countess Geschwitz and Alwa Schön; Geschwitz's row is derived by extracting every fifth note from the source row and Alwa's by extracting every seventh note.[10] These rows also fit Reich's description in that every third note of Geschwitz's row is identical with every third note of the source row, and every second note of Alwa's row is identical with every second note of the source row (Example 29).

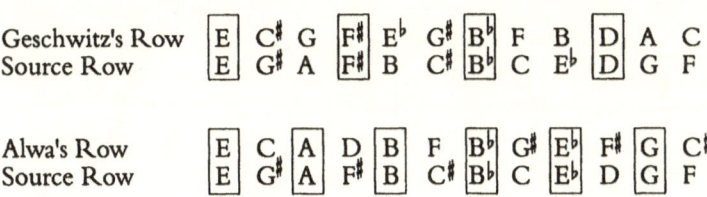

EXAMPLE 29.   Invariant properties of Geschwitz's row and Alwa's row

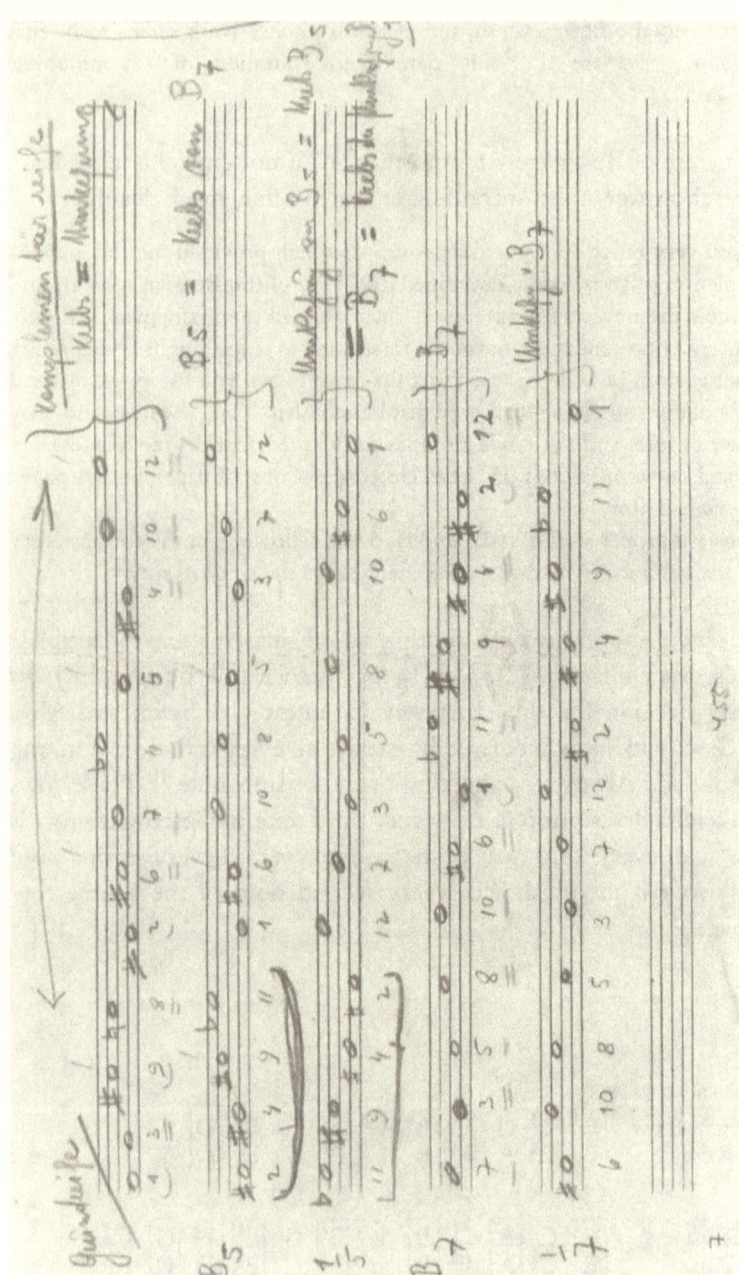

FIGURE 35. Reich's row sketch showing the derivation of B_5 and B_7. ÖNB Musiksammlung F 21 Berg 28/XI, fol. 7т

112   Berg's Tone Rows for Lulu

During my study at the Nationalbibliothek I discovered the row sketch that accompanied Reich's letter, mixed among Berg's sketches for *Lulu* (Figure 35). As Reich explains in his letter, the point of the sketch is to show what properties result when Berg's B_5 and B_7 operations are applied to a complementary series. On staff 1 Reich has written a source row that he labels with pitch-class numbers 1 through 12, with 1 designating F. To the right he notes that it is a "Komplementärreihe" and that its retrograde is identical to its inversion. On staves 2 and 4 Reich applies Berg's B_5 and B_7 operations to the source row. If one compares the newly derived rows to the original, it is apparent that, indeed, B_5 is constructed by extracting every fifth note from the source row and B_7 by extracting every seventh note (Example 30). Reich also indicates the invariant pitches between the source row and its transformations; every third note of B_5 and the source row is marked with vertical slashes and every second note of B_7 and the source row is marked with a horizontal double slash. Finally, he writes out on staves 3 and 5 an inversional form of B_5 and B_7. The main property of the source row (that is, that its retrograde is equivalent to its inversion) is retained in the newly derived rows B_5 and B_7. Furthermore, because the retrograde of B_5 will always be identical to B_7, a new link exists: $I(B_5) = R(B_5) = B_7 = RI(B_7)$.

The B_5 and B_7 operations shown in Reich's row sketch still differ slightly from the row permutations that Berg uses in *Lulu*. Whereas Reich's derived rows begin with the fifth and seventh note of the source row, Berg, in the B_5 and B_7 rows for *Lulu*, begins with the first note of the source row and only then extracts every fifth or seventh note. One of the row sketches for *Lulu*, however, shows that Berg did in fact originally

EXAMPLE 30. Derivation of B_5 and B_7 from Reich's complementary row

FIGURE 36. Early row sketch showing the derivation of B_5 and B_7 from the source row for *Lulu*. ÖNB Musiksammlung F 21 Berg 28/XXIII, fol. 3r

generate B_5 and B_7 just as they appear in Reich's row sketch (Figure 36). Here Berg, using the same technique, has written out the source row for *Lulu* (staff 1) and then selectively extracted every fifth note (staves 3–5) and every seventh note (staves 6–8). The order numbers written below the source row (staves 3–5 and 6–8) indicate the sequence of pitches for the newly derived rows. Next to the sketch Berg notes: "From this source row (and every twelve-tone row) one can form two (and *only* two) new twelve-tone rows if one *systematically* extracts tones. That is, if one (1) extracts every fifth pitch and (2) extracts every seventh pitch.[11]

In a nearly identical sketch (Figure 37) Berg now retains the first note of the source row for *Lulu*, then systematically extracts every fifth note (staves 2–3) and every seventh note (staves 4–7). Below the sketch is a lengthy note that reveals the reason for Berg's fascination with B_5 and B_7: they represent the only exact patterns of extraction through which one can build a new twelve-tone row.[12] He explains:

With every other row derivation of this type (whether one extracts every second, third, fourth, or sixth tone), rows with fewer (up to two) tones are formed, because sooner or later the tones begin to repeat. If one extracts every eighth, ninth, or tenth tone, the retrograde form of these 2–6-tone rows is formed. They are, therefore, unusable. Whereas the other rows (the only ones) are indeed completely new rows, but are still closely and [missing word] related to the source row. That they are organically related to the former is evident from the fact that when one extracts every eleventh note (which has not yet happened here), the retrograde of the source row is formed (naturally!), which closes the circle.[13]

This annotation makes clear that for Berg, "unity with the source row" means subsidiary rows formed by exact patterns of extraction. Because the interval of extraction for the other possible derivations (every second, third, fourth, and sixth note) divides evenly into twelve, only six notes, at most, can be extracted before repetitions occur (Example 31). This clarifies Reich's statement to Berg in his letter of September 21: "The reason that *only* the fifth, seventh, and eleventh pitches work seems to be that 1 + 11 and 5 + 7 are the only pure prime numbers of 12."

FIGURE 37. Later row sketch of B_5 and B_7. ÖNB Musiksammlung F 21 Berg 28/XI, fol. 1r

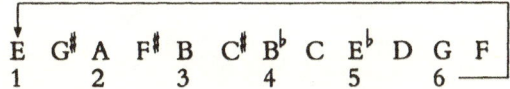

EXAMPLE 31. Pitch duplication in a "B_2" row

On the verso side of the same sketch (Figure 38) Berg works through every possible uniform pattern of extraction and assigns four of the resulting rows to characters in *Lulu*. For the patterns that divide equally into twelve, and thus generate rows of only two to six tones, Berg uses a slight modification of his cyclic procedure. He contrives to form rows by extracting every second and third note, for instance, by shifting to the next available note when a pitch is repeated.[14] The rows formed in this manner are labeled "Rodrigo" and "Hugenberg."[15] Berg notes that Rodrigo needed one break in the cyclic method and Hugenberg, two. The rows formed by extracting every fifth and seventh note are assigned to Countess Geschwitz and Alwa. Berg calls these "correct new rows"; that is, it is not necessary to break the cyclic pattern in order to form them.

As we recall from Chapter 4, Berg also derives Dr. Schön's row (not listed on the sketch sheet) by a cyclic procedure.[16] He uses a palindromic pattern to extract notes from the source row, first skipping one note, then two, then three, then the reverse — three notes, two notes, and one (Example 32).

Now that the nature of Berg's discovery is clear, we are better able to understand his letter to Schoenberg from September 1, 1928:

> Your interest in my new opera also makes me happy, and I take your suggestions no less seriously than those you gave me 20 years ago. I believe I am following them *in that* I'm not restricting myself to a *single* row, but have from the outset derived *from it* a number of *other* forms (scale forms, chromatic, fourth and third forms, progressions of triads and tetrachords, etc., etc., etc.), which I then interpret (each one) as an independent row and *treat* as such (with all of its inversions and retrograde forms). Always retaining the right, — in case that doesn't suffice: to construct a *new* row, as I did in my *Lyric Suite,* where the row underwent small changes with each pair of movements (through the *reordering* of a few pitches), which at least back then was very stimulating while working.

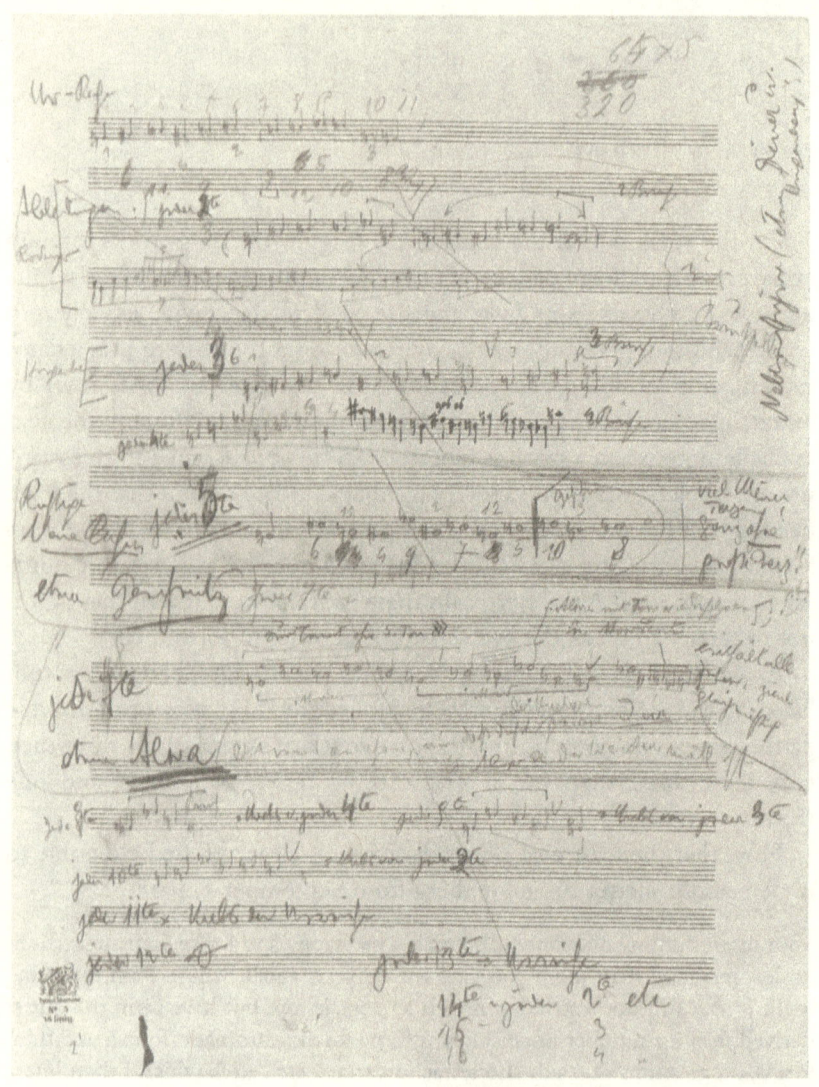

FIGURE 38. Sketch showing derivation of various cyclic rows for *Lulu*. ÖNB Musiksammlung F 21 Berg 28/XI, fol. 1v

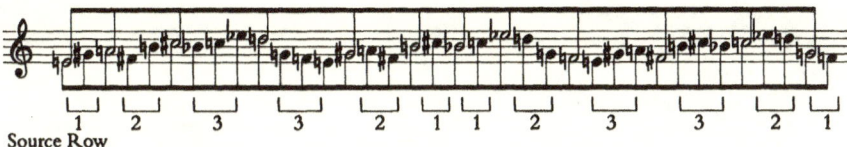

EXAMPLE 32. Derivation of Dr. Schön's row from the source row

But such decisions need not be made for a long time yet: Although I have already composed over 300 measures, that's a mere beginning for an opera of over 3,000 measures. And to think of what fate may have in store for these plans of mine—despite the most rigorous planning—in the course of the years of work ahead![17]

The rows that Berg describes here—scale forms, chromatic forms, fourth and third forms, and so forth—are listed with their transpositions and inversions on the large row chart for *Lulu* cited in Chapter 2, dated July 17, 1927 (Figure 39; summarized in Example 33).[18] It is these forms that Berg was referring to in his letter to Webern of September 20, 1929, when he wrote about "the various forms that I had already derived for it [*Lulu*] long ago." Many of these forms are associated with characters or events in the first two scenes of the opera: the chromatic form (Example 33h) is assigned to Schigolch and the scale form (Example 33e), to Lulu; the three-note chords (Example 33d) become the Bild Harmonien; the third form (Example 33f) appears with the death of the Medical Advisor. In general, Berg derives the rows listed on this chart by rearranging or selectively grouping notes from a single statement of the source row. The rows from 1929, in contrast, are derived by the new procedure of systematically extracting notes from successive statements of the source row. Thus they represent a later and distinct stage in Berg's row derivation for *Lulu*.

A second interesting point in Berg's letter to Schoenberg is that he has completed more than three hundred measures of the opera. If so, one might expect a detectable break in his compositional method when he began incorporating the new rows derived by the 1929 method. The *Particell* and early drafts for Act I, scenes 1–2, do, in fact, show clearly where the break took place. Moreover, Berg's penchant for writing drafts of

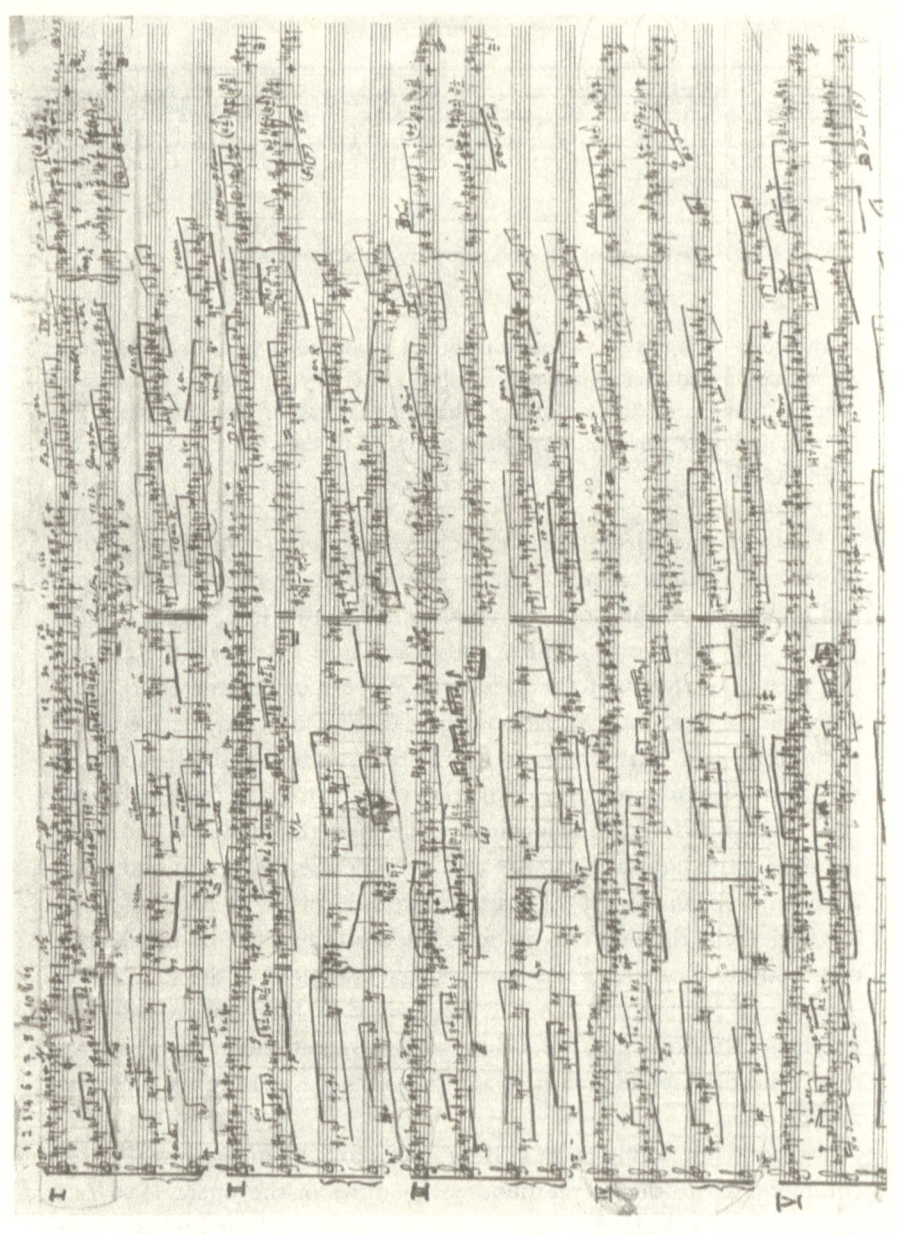

FIGURE 20 Row chart for *Lulu* dated July 17, 1927. ÖNB Musiksammlung F 21 Berg 28/L (upper left section)

EXAMPLE 33. Partial transcription of F 21 Berg 28/L (see Figure 39)

(continued)

EXAMPLE 33, *continued*

letters while he sketched allows us to date the break fairly accurately as September 1929.[19] The music of *Lulu*, from Alwa's tentative "May I come in?" at the opening of Act I, scene 1, to Dr. Schön's stormy entrance in the following scene (m. 523), derives entirely from the earlier method. The two exceptions, Alwa's row in mm. 98–99 and Dr. Schön's row in mm. 119–23, are not present in the earlier drafts; it is only in the finished *Particell* that they appear, and one can see from the overlay where they have been grafted onto the original.

Figure 40, a *Particell* section from the opening of scene 1 (mm. 118–24), shows the second of these grafted passages. Alwa and Schön have been conversing with Lulu while the Painter works on her portrait. Schön's comment to the Painter—"You must work a little more from the model. The hair is bad. You aren't paying enough attention"—is accompanied in the original *Particell* layer (written in ink) by an inversional form of the Bild Harmonien (Example 34a). At a later point, Berg carefully added Schön's row in pencil, in the form of his "Gewaltmensch" theme from the Sonata music. The only major revision, the vocal line in mm. 122–23, doubles one segment of the series (Example 34b). As a stage cue to Schön's entrance, Berg adds: "With the clear intention of diverting."

If we compare the two versions, it is striking that in the second one Schön's personality suddenly comes to life. By using Schön's own theme and row form, Berg is now able to distinguish him musically from the other characters, and consequently the passage becomes dramatically more effective.

Sketches like these, which show the juxtaposition of Berg's derivational methods, make us more aware of how Berg's twelve-tone technique evolved—and this is really one of the most significant ideas we can gain from his discovery. Berg composed *Lulu* over a span of seven years, and we know from studying the opera's chronology that his work suffered extended interruptions during this time. It is not surprising, then, that *Lulu* shows distinct stages reflecting changes in Berg's compositional technique. Without the sketches and drafts, these stages—perhaps slightly camouflaged through "touch-ups" like the one described above —could easily remain undetected.

But more important, Berg's sketches allow us finally to put to rest the one-row controversy—the debate regarding Berg's claim that the music

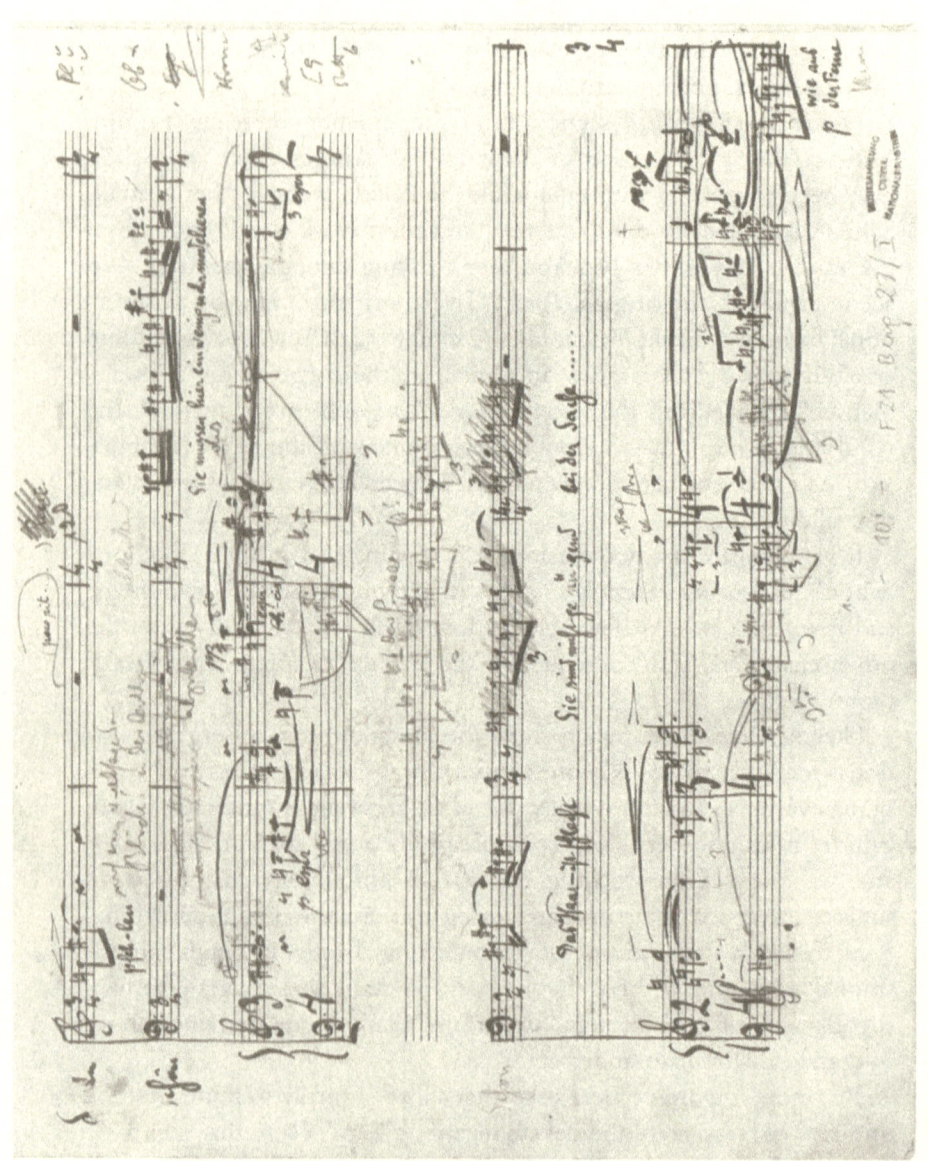

of *Lulu* is unified through his use of a single row to derive all subsidiary rows, and the important exchange between Reich and Perle.[20] As I remarked in Chapter 4, Perle maintains that the relationship between most of the subsidiary rows and the source row (self-evident from Berg's row charts) is never established in the music itself; thus one cannot assume that these subsidiary rows guarantee aesthetic unity.[21] Yet we still do not know what Berg *did* mean by his statement, and even the many row operations Reich cited in defense of Berg's claim fail to provide this information.

Berg's sketches and correspondence show clearly that he felt *Lulu* was unified through the "organic relationship" he had worked out between the cyclic rows and the source row—namely, that the cyclic rows could be derived from the source row without shifts or breaks (as with Alwa, Geschwitz, and Schön's rows) or with minimal breaks (as with the Schoolboy and the Acrobat's rows). Ironically, Berg never felt the need to use this elaborate justification for the 1927 precyclic rows; in his sketches he simply states that they are derived "direct" from the source row.[22]

Although Berg's new technique for deriving rows represents a distinct stage in *Lulu*, we should not lose sight of its place in the evolution of Berg's row technique. In the *Violin Concerto*, composed from late April though July 1935, Berg continues to experiment with new methods of row transformation, and had he lived, his row techniques would undoubtedly have developed even further. In *Lulu*, Berg focused for several years on one aspect of this development in order to deal with both the sheer length of the opera and its challenging dramatic requirements.

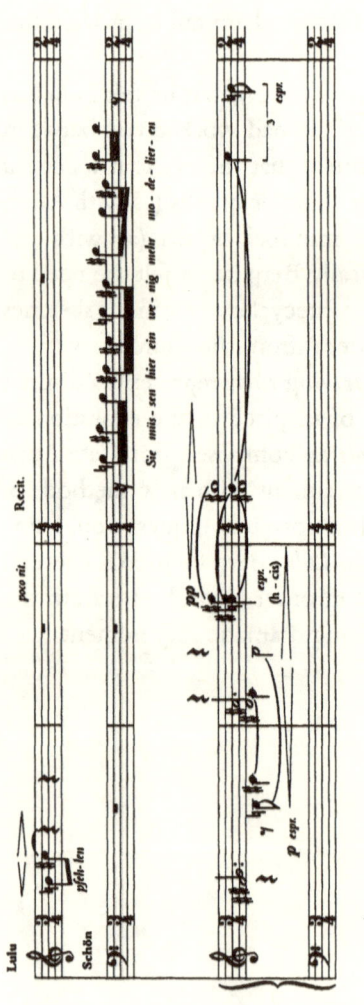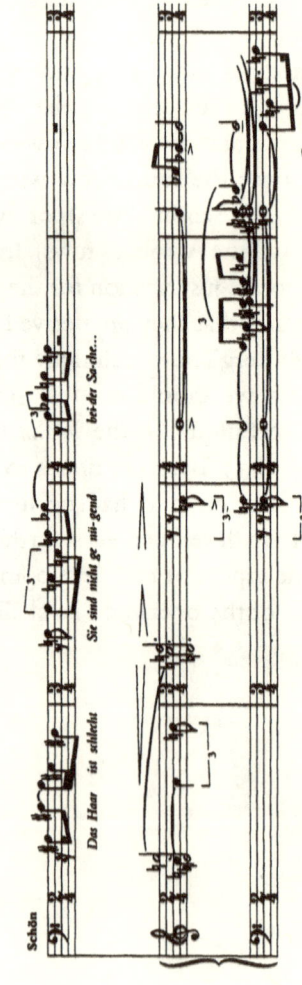

EXAMPLE 34A. Transcription of F 21 Berg 29/I, fol. 12r, mm. 118–24, original layer (see Figure 40)

EXAMPLE 34B. Transcription of F 21 Berg 29/I, fol. 12r, mm. 118–24, original plus added layer (order numbers added; see Figure 40)

Berg's Tone Rows for Lulu   127

Chapter 6

Why Is Berg's Twelve-Tone Music So Difficult to Analyze?

In his essay "Why Is Schoenberg's Music So Difficult to Understand?" Berg argues that the average listener fails to comprehend Schoenberg's music, not because the language is novel, but because it combines many richly developed compositional techniques used by the masters of the past:

Think of Bach's polyphony; of the structure of the themes—often quite free constructionally and rhythmically, of the classical and pre-classical composers, and of their highly skilled treatment of the principle of variation; of the Romantics, with their bold juxtapositions (which are still bold even today) of distantly related keys; of the new chordal formations in Wagner arrived at by chromatic alteration and enharmonic change, and their natural embodiment in tonality; and finally think of Brahms' art of thematic and motivic work, often penetrating into the very smallest details.

It is clear that a music that unites in itself all these possibilities that the masters of the past have left behind would not only be *different* from a contemporary music where such a combination is not to be found (as I will show); it also—despite those properties that we recognized as the merits of good music, and despite its excessive richness in all the fields of music, or rather, just *because* of this—it also manages to be difficult to understand, which indeed Schoenberg's music is.[1]

Berg might have made a similar claim about the music of *Lulu*. For although the thematic quality of its twelve-tone rows and the latent tonality of its harmonies make the opera somewhat more comprehensible, they mask a complexity that is due, like Schoenberg's, to the simultaneous use and interaction of many involved compositional parameters. These include the multiple levels of dramatic symbolism, the formation of the music to conform to the text, the interaction of smaller forms with the overall palindromic structure of the opera, the network of motivic and thematic coherence, the frequent tonal allusion, and, finally, Berg's decision to express these parameters using the twelve-tone method.

While the secondary literature includes many penetrating analyses of *Lulu*, they frequently reflect at least two weaknesses: first, they often leave very difficult passages unanalyzed (simply because these passages sometimes make such rudimentary information as order numbers and row forms equivocal); and second, they sometimes minimize, or even dismiss, factors that are essential to understanding the music's function. Such omissions are critical, since Berg's music shows, not only an interaction, but also a precarious balance between his twelve-tone method and the above textual and musical parameters. Thus, seemingly "imprecise" orderings of pitches, complex methods of row derivation, and other unusual techniques of composing often represent Berg's manipulation of the twelve-tone method to accommodate dramatic symbolism, motivic adherence, and tonality.

In this final chapter, then, I discuss the most immediate level of the opera, Berg's twelve-tone technique, as an expression of other relevant textual and musical properties. After introducing sketches pertaining to form and dramatic symbolism, I focus primarily on compositional sketches and drafts of selected passages from each act of the opera to illustrate specific aspects of Berg's twelve-tone technique. I have chosen sketches for these particular passages because few detailed analyses of them exist in the secondary literature (no doubt because theorists are daunted by their complexity); moreover, many of these sketches reveal features of Berg's twelve-tone technique that are especially difficult to ascertain from the finished score. Since Berg's later techniques of composing are often developments of earlier ones, I shall progress through these passages chronologically, emphasizing the evolution of Berg's twelve-tone method that I set forth in Chapter 2.

FIGURE 41 (*above and opposite*).
Draft of the opening of Act I, scene 1.
ÖNB Musiksammlung F 21 Berg
28/XXIV, fols. 2v–3r.

I begin by analyzing in some detail the opening of the first scene, which, as we recall from Chapter 1, is the first passage of the opera that Berg retained in the final version. Berg's draft of this passage appears as Figure 41, summarized in Example 35. Here we return to a style that is almost

Why Is Berg's Music Difficult to Analyze?

EXAMPLE 35 (*above and following pages*).
Partial transcription of F 21 Berg
28/XXIV, fols. 2v–3r

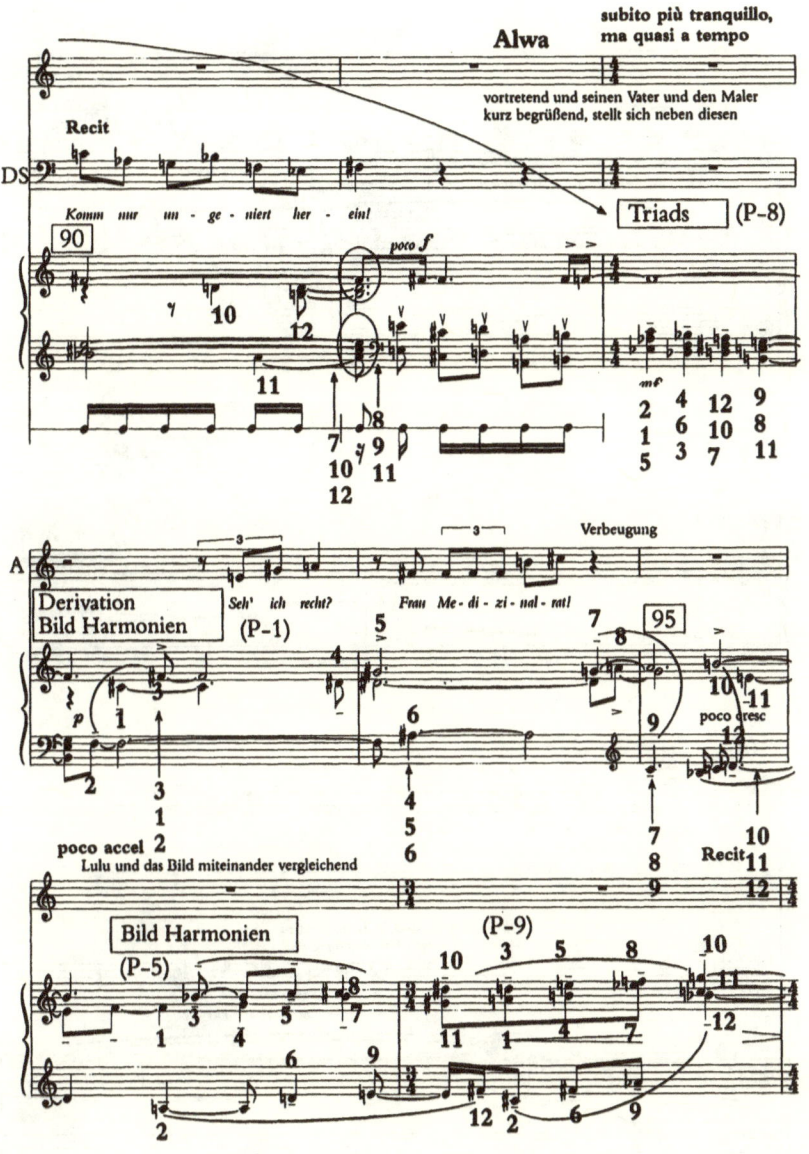

EXAMPLE 35, *continued*

134   *Why Is Berg's Music Difficult to Analyze?*

reminiscent of the *Lyric Suite,* one that precedes the innovations of *Der Wein.* It is also the least complicated passage that I analyze in this chapter; yet, as we shall see, the sketches offer crucial insights about its twelve-tone organization.

The first of these insights derives simply from our knowledge of chronology: since we know that this passage was composed in 1928, we need only refer to Berg's row chart from 1927 to identify which of the thirteen possible row forms he is using. Or we can examine the sketch itself, for in it Berg identifies not only the row forms but also their respective configurations and operations (transposition, inversion, or retrogression), which in the draft shown in Figure 41 appear as annotations in the margins or between the staves.[2] While Berg's relatively simple style of composing at the beginning of this scene makes the identification of some row forms unambiguous, it is often more direct (as well as accurate) to rely on his numerous annotations and row charts. Moreover, specific configurations of the source row, such as the triadic form shown in Example 36, are rarely cited in the theoretical literature. Consequently, passages using these configurations would most likely be analyzed as "unstructured" or "free."

A second insight, which results from Berg's annotations of musical function, helps us evaluate preexisting theories about how the music works—for many properties that analysts have taken great care to hypothesize are in fact immediately apparent from Berg's draft. Manfred Reiter, for instance, uses Berg's initial statements of subsidiary rows that appear in this passage as fodder for the one-row controversy. Citing the four triads that Berg extracts from the inverted form of the source row (mm. 86–91), Reiter argues: "The principle through which these chords are employed, and whether they derive from the source row, is a question of particular interest at this point. For the first occurrence of the harmonic configuration [triads] is presented here as a compositional process."[3]

Later, in reference to the statements of the Bild Harmonien in mm. 93–97, he comments:

The process through which the Bild Harmonien are introduced here is significant. In contrast to the passage mentioned by Reich, where they appear as a completed row derivation, here they are generated before the ears of the listener; for they successively crystallize out of a VD [vertical dodecaphonic] arrangement of the source row in the high strings, until finally—the third time

EXAMPLE 36. Triadic form of the source row

EXAMPLE 37. Summary of the derivation of the triads (mm. 86–91)

EXAMPLE 38. Summary of the derivation of the Bild Harmonien (mm. 93–97)

(m. 97), with the entrance of the clarinets, they are stabilized into their chord form. Therefore, the derivation of the Bild Harmonien of the source row takes place in a compositional manner.[4]

In the left-hand margin of fol. 2v Berg writes, "die 4 Dreiklänge (im Entstehung)" (genesis of the four triads); between staves 7 and 8 of m. 93 he writes, "3 Klang Akkorde im Entstehung" (genesis of the trichords). These derivations are labeled in Example 35 and summarized in Examples 37 and 38. These annotations recall, of course, the sketches that I discuss in Chapter 4 of the derivation of Dr. Schön's row, where Berg makes nearly identical annotations. This draft reveals, then, that Berg consciously articulates the derivation of these subsidiary rows from the source row during their first appearance in the music. These unfoldings (as I note in Chapter 4) differ from those in the Sonata in that they are local events whose principal function is to demonstrate the relation of the subsidiary row to the source row. They are not complex statements of dramatic symbolism, for nothing in the text justifies such a function.

We can, in addition, glean a few other ideas from Berg's annotations. For instance, what is the significance of Berg's arrow (left-hand margin of fol. 2v) that connects the inverted and prime forms of the triad configuration? Although Berg is perhaps less explicit here than in his other annotations, the arrow nonetheless suggests a progression from the inverted form of the triad configuration to its transposed prime form or, more accurately, a type of closure—for the rows that take part in the progression are the same.[5] Berg uses a similar technique in mm. 98–102, where he moves from the fourths form (prime), to an intervening row (the whole-tone form), and back to the fourths form in inversion. Again, the reason for Berg's use of closure undoubtedly lies in the text. The opening of the opera features a rather introductory, loosely structured, text—yet there are certainly self-contained sections, which Berg "frames" and thus articulates with the same row forms. For instance, the dialogue concerning Alwa's entrance—"May I come in?" "My son!" "That is Herr Alwa!" "Please come in!"—is separated from the next portion of dialogue, in which Alwa turns his attention to Lulu. In addition, Berg creates melodic tension with the drawn-out ascending melodic line of these configurations, which is then resolved by their rhythmically diminished descending form (see Example 35).

A final insight derives not simply from Berg's annotations themselves, but from the clarity with which he lays out his musical ideas in the draft. Compare, for instance, Berg's notation of the fourths form and its inversion, discussed above (mm. 98–99 and 101–2 of the draft), with the same progression in the printed piano-vocal score (Example 35). In the score, the progression is obscured by the split beaming and separation into two clefs. Furthermore, notice in the draft how clearly Berg shows the relationship between the fourths form and the whole-tone form (mm. 98–100), in which the whole-tone form nearly duplicates the upper line of the fourths form. Thus, Berg's draft reveals two different row forms expressing nearly identical musical content—a relationship that (in this instance) is concealed in the final score.

EXAMPLE 39. Duet of Act I, scene 1 (mm. 305–8)

Before I begin a second analysis, let me briefly summarize the techniques of twelve-tone composition in the draft discussed above: (1) Berg's conscious demonstration of the relation between subsidiary rows and the source row, (2) his use of closure to create discrete sections that articulate the structure of the text, and (3) his use of two different row forms to express nearly identical musical material. In addition, Berg's annotations, as well as his row charts, completed a year before he composed the draft, allow us to identify more precisely the many row configurations.

The second passage is from the Duet of Act I, scene 1. To my knowledge, it has never been analyzed in the secondary literature (Example 39) —undoubtedly because of the complexity of Berg's twelve-tone technique that marks this section of the opera. The dramatic action of the Duet is as follows: after Lulu's indifferent reaction to the death of her first husband, the Medical Advisor, the Painter initiates a question-and-answer session, which he begins by asking Lulu, "Kannst Du die Wahrheit sagen?" (Can you speak the truth?). To each of the Painter's questions, Lulu simply answers, "Ich weiss es nicht" (I don't know).

The text for this passage is based on a single repeated idea: the Painter's question and Lulu's response. At the same time, however, there is a progressive heightening of the dramatic tension with each question and answer that reflects the increasing exasperation of both the Painter and Lulu. And as always, Berg finds a perfect musical vehicle to articulate the textual form, for his sketches show that he chose the theme and variation. Thus, the repetition of each variation emphasizes the repetition of the textual idea; the successive elaboration reflects the emotional heightening portrayed in the drama.

If we were to analyze the passage without the aid of Berg's sketches, we would probably notice—from both the melodic line and the previous few bars—that he uses the Bild Harmonien (Example 40). But the

EXAMPLE 40. Bild Harmonien

FIGURE 42. Sketch of the Duet, Act I, scene 2 (mm. 302–14). ÖNB Musiksammlung F 21 Berg 28/XXIV fol. 13v

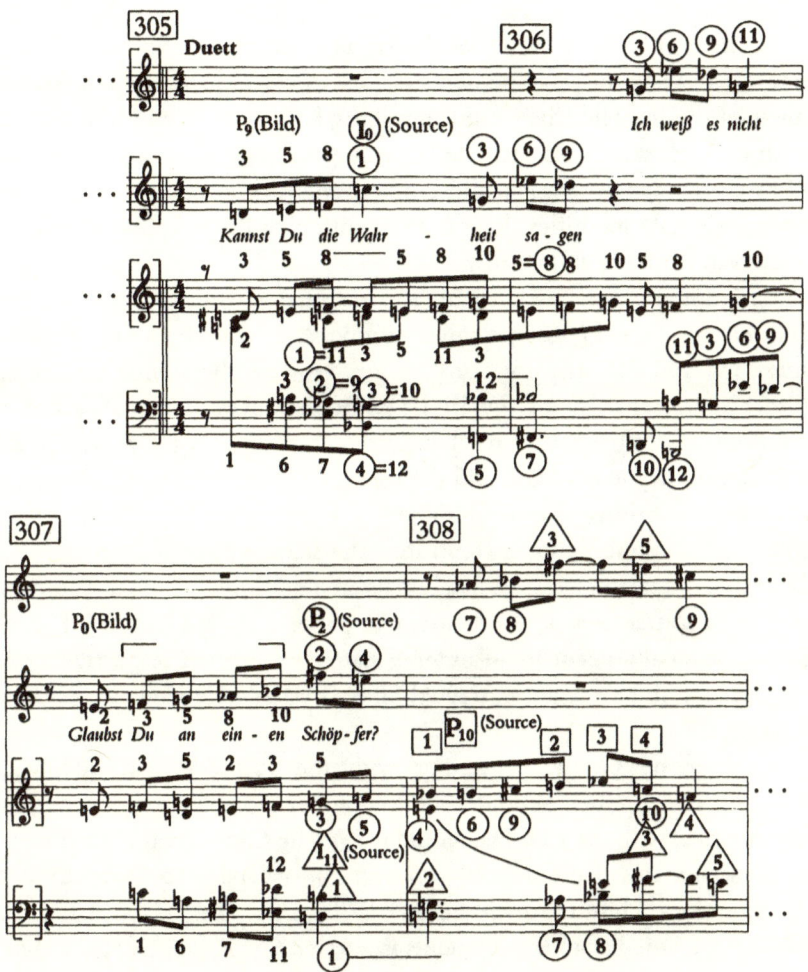

EXAMPLE 41. Summary transcription of F 21 Berg 28/XXIV, fol. 13v

second half of the Painter's vocal line (C, G, E flat, D flat) is more difficult to analyze, for it does not form a recognizable segment of any of Berg's twelve-tone rows. This vocal line, and the even more complex passage in measure 308, might make us suspect that Berg dispenses with his conventional twelve-tone operations, and that thus his writing becomes structurally "free"; however, if we look at Berg's compositional sketches for the passage (one of which appears as Figure 42, summarized in Example 41), we see that, on the contrary, Berg derives all the notes from two different row forms.

In the sketch, Berg identifies the occurrence of specific twelve-tone rows in a variety of ways: he uses brackets to mark off a complete statement of the row; he labels order numbers; he uses Roman numerals (as with the first sketch) to indicate the transpositional level and the letters O or U to indicate Original and Umkehrung (prime and inversion); and he occasionally identifies the exact derivation of the row, that is, how it is derived from the source row.

As I noted earlier, the first phrase, measures 305–6, begins with the Bild Harmonien (P_9). Berg's order numbers in the second half of measures 305 and 306 identify our "mystery" row as the source row at I_0 (order numbers 9–12 of the Bild Harmonien overlapping with order numbers 1–4 of the source row). Berg does not identify the repeating E, F, G figures in measure 306 and the second half of measure 305 because they are repetitions of order numbers 5, 8, 10 of the Bild Harmonien. (Notice that these figures extend into the statement of source row I_0.) Likewise, the unlabeled G, E flat, D flats are repetitions of order numbers 3, 6, 9 of source row I_0. Both melodic patterns, E, F, G and G, E flat, D flat, originally occur in an ordered statement of their respective rows (P_9 and I_0) and are then extracted and stated as independent melodic fragments.[6]

The second phrase, beginning with the Painter's next question, "Glaubst Du an einen Schöpfer?" (Do you believe in a Creator?), begins like the first, with the Bild Harmonien (P_0). The three ordered statements of the source row that follow (P_2, I_{11}, and P_{10}) are spliced to form distinct melodic lines. Thus, the melodic line B flat, B, C sharp, D, E flat, C, A (piano) is formed from the segments P_{10}: 1; P_2: 6, 9; P_{10}: 2, 3, 4; I_{11}: 4. The vocal line A flat, B flat, F sharp, E, C sharp is formed from P_2: 7, 8; I_{11}: 3, 5; P_2: 9. Berg reveals this splicing in his sketch by placing the order numbers for each row in separate layers. Notice that Berg is again extracting segments from ordered statements and expressing them as melodic fragments; I refer here to the A flat, B flat, F sharp, E in the piano part, measure 308, which derives from the vocal line of that same measure.

With this basic level of analysis conquered, we can reach for more creative realms. Specifically, we can begin to understand the reasons—both musical and dramatic—for some of Berg's more complicated row manipulations. For instance, Berg's E, F, G figure, which extends into source row I_0 (measures 305–6), functions as a bridge to the next phrase, which also begins with E, F, G. Notice that Berg expresses these segments using different rows and order numbers: the statements of E, F, G in phrase 1 are formed from order numbers 5, 8, 10 of Bild Harmonien P_9 and the E, F, G that opens phrase 2 from order numbers 2, 3, 5 of Bild Harmonien P_0. Berg's wish to repeat previous melodic figures while using different rows and order numbers also explains the spliced melodic line of measure 308. Compare, for instance, the A flat, B flat, F sharp, E in the vocal line of measure 307 (Bild Harmonien P_0: 8, 10, source row P_2: 2, 4) with the identical A flat, B flat, F sharp, E segment of the vocal line in measure 308. With this technique, Berg, using contrasting row material, achieves the same continuity as he does by merely repeating a row segment literally—as in the first phrase, where he takes the latter part of the Painter's vocal line, G, E flat, D flat, and repeats it twice as a melodic fragment. This technique, of course, serves to articulate the structure of the text, for the echoing effect of the two similar segments reminds us that this is indeed a question and answer. Note also that the second segment, A flat, B flat, F sharp, E, is an elaboration of the first melodic segment, G, E flat, D flat, and thus emphasizes the emotional heightening and variation form.

In this short example, sketches have allowed us to unravel highly complicated aspects of Berg's compositional style that might otherwise remain hidden or ambiguous: Berg's splicing of two different row forms or his reordering of a single row to express previous motivic material. In addition, Berg interpolates pitches from other rows to express motivic elaboration.

I turn now to the Rondo of Act II. In contrast to my previous analyses, however, I examine, not a single passage, but sketches from various sections of the Rondo. In the context of this discussion I also comment on certain similarities between the Rondo and the Sonata discussed in Chapter 4. Before investigating details of Berg's twelve-tone technique, I begin with some general comments about the overall form of the Rondo. Example 42 summarizes its form, using the nomenclature and theme division appearing in Berg's sketches.

Like the Sonata of Act I, the Rondo encompasses an entire act; its exposition takes place in Act II, scene 1, and its development and reprise in Act II, scene 2. While the Sonata represents Dr. Schön, the Rondo depicts his son, Alwa. But the themes of the Rondo, unlike those of the

Exposition (Act II, scene 1)

Main theme (A_1), mm. 243–49

Bridge theme, mm. 262–65

Subsidiary theme (B) mm. 266–73, 275–80

Main theme (A_2) and Bridge, mm. 281–86, 298–306

Coda themes (C_1) mm. 306–9, (C_1 and C_2) mm. 318–37

Development (Act II, scene 2)
mm. 1001–58

Reprise (Act II, scene 2)
mm. 1059–1150

EXAMPLE 42.   Form and thematic division of the Rondo

Sonata, represent, not different characters, but different facets of Alwa's personality and his love for Lulu.[7] Berg reflects this difference in symbolism in his construction of his themes; while the four themes of the Sonata seem intentionally to contrast in character, those of the Rondo are more homogeneous—even to the extent that the A_I and C_2 themes are actually variants of each other (Example 43).[8] Note that A_I is essentially a fragmented, less conclusive statement of C_2. Thus, when Berg's C_2 theme occurs in the coda of the Rondo, it in a sense "completes" the A theme, so that the coda functions as the Rondo's climax. Dramatically, it is the climax, for here Alwa finally admits to Lulu that he loves her. It is thus the dramatic counterpart of the coda of the Sonata, where Lulu professes her love for Dr. Schön.

The idea of large-scale completion, while supported by the dramatic action and construction of themes, was originally suggested to me by one of Berg's annotations in the *Particell*.[9] In this annotation, he explains that Alwa's vocal delivery is constructed to form a gradual "Steigerung" (intensification), from speaking without musical accompaniment (introduction), to speaking with musical accompaniment (A section), to *Sprechstimme*, to singing parlando, and finally to singing cantabile in the "Eine Seele" theme of the coda. Berg uses this same gradual intensification of vocal delivery in the coda of the Sonata, however, on a much smaller scale.

EXAMPLE 43. Comparison of A_1 and C_2 themes of the Rondo

The use or exclusion of tonal allusion also plays an important role in large-scale completion. It has gradually become clear to me, from both Berg's sketches and his music, how he consciously controls the amount of tonality present. While in some passages tonality is thwarted, in others it predominates. Tonal allusion often predominates in extended climactic passages to emphasize musically a sense of arrival; this is true in the coda of the Sonata and, of course, in the coda of the Rondo. I discuss Berg's use of this technique in more detail in a later section.

Perhaps the many interruptions—both between and within themes—are the most obvious reason for the unrequited character of the A and B sections. Dramatically, these interpretations occur because Alwa pours out his innermost feelings to Lulu while being secretly observed by the Schoolboy, Countess Geschwitz, the Athlete, and his insanely jealous father. In addition to two interruptions by the Manservant, there are three enraged asides by Dr. Schön and an aborted escape by the Athlete. It is only in the coda that one has the sense that Alwa has finally "delivered the message," but even here he is interrupted by his father (in person rather than as a dramatic aside), and the Rondo abruptly breaks off until the following scene, when Lulu returns to the same setting after escaping from prison. In both the Sonata and the Rondo, Berg interrupts the form at the end of the exposition, delaying the development and reprise until the following scene. These two halves of the Rondo occur in the two center scenes of the opera, and thus contribute to its overall palindromic structure, discussed in Chapter 3. And like the themes of the Rondo, its reprise has a much more circuitous character than the Sonata; Alwa's feelings for Lulu are the same as in the exposition, despite her now being an emaciated cholera victim. Alwa, like so many of Lulu's admirers, is fixated on an image, rather than a real person. This fixation reaches its pathetic apex in the Quartet of the final scene, where Lulu is a wretched prostitute, and Alwa, Geschwitz, and Schigolch sing fragments of the Rondo while gazing, not at Lulu, but at her portrait. Thus, while the Sonata features an elaborate plot, in which Schön finally succumbs to Lulu, the Rondo is actionless and centers on a state of mind.

In true Bergian style, the Rondo is infused with dramatic symbolism. Berg was, of course, fascinated with the major-minor relationship that he had inadvertently created through his numeric derivation of Dr. Schön's and Alwa's rows. It symbolizes not only their familial relationship, but also the conflict between them that arises from their love for Lulu. For instance, Berg notes in the *Particell* that Alwa's minor triad inverts to become major in Act II, scene 2, suggesting that Alwa, now Lulu's lover, has assumed his father's previous role.

A second conflict depicted in the music is within Alwa himself, for he and Lulu have grown up "as brother and sister"; thus, in addition to challenging his father, he must somehow surmount the barrier of "brotherly love." Berg expresses this conflict by alternating between "erotic" and "spiritual" musical themes. For instance, in a form sketch for the Rondo, shown in Figure 43, Berg identifies the dramatic flavor of each dialogue between Alwa and Lulu, and its accompanying musical theme (enclosed in octagons). He notes that the dialogue after Schigolch's exit (accompanied by the A theme) is erotic. Here he specifies that Lulu appear in "a low-cut ball gown" and that she ask Alwa, "How do you like me?" The dialogue after the transition, accompanied by the B theme, is "spiritual" ("You were always like a brother. You are the only man in the world who protected me"). And the dialogue after Schön's interruption (mm. 273–74), which, Berg notes, is to be accompanied by both the A and B themes, is both "erotic and spiritual." At the bottom of the sketch, Berg again outlines Alwa's types of vocal delivery in the Rondo, which effect the large-scale completion in the coda.

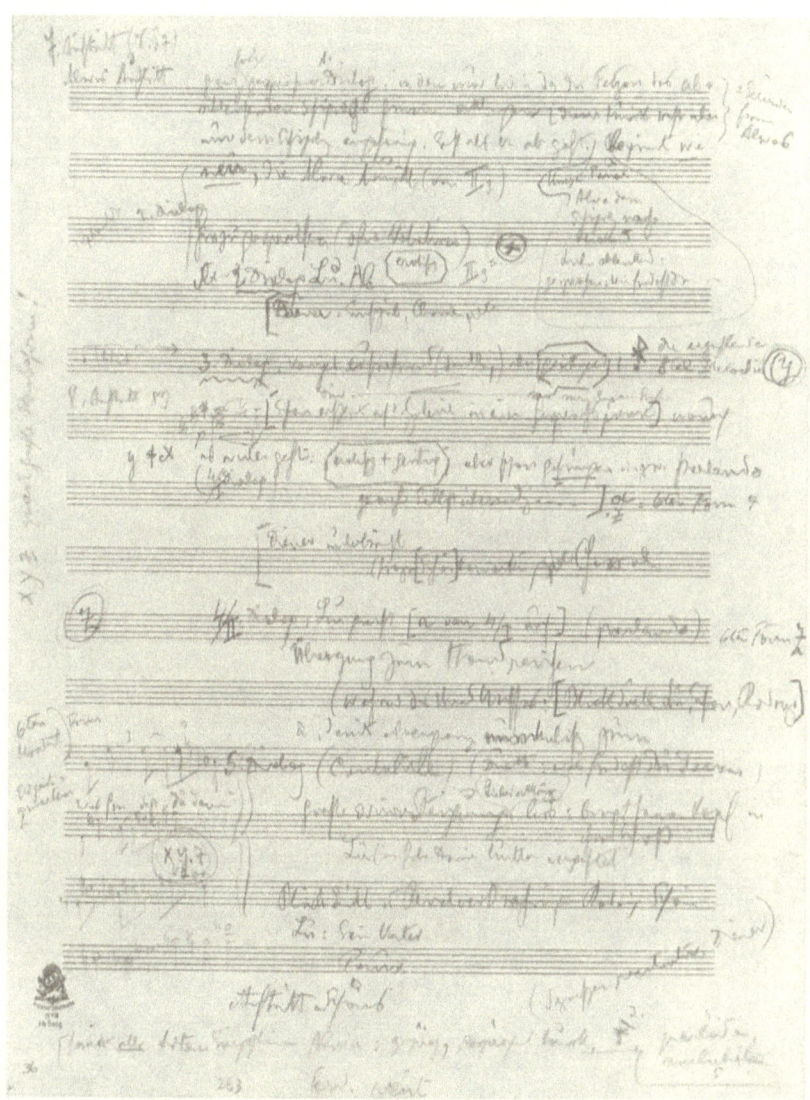

FIGURE 43. Sketch of form and dramatic symbolism for the Rondo. ÖNB Musiksammlung F 21 Berg 28/XXXVII, fol. 36r

FIGURE 44. Row chart for Alwa's row. ÖNB Musiksammlung F 21 Berg 28/XVII, fol. 17r

EXAMPLE 44.   Extraction of Erdgeist fourths from the source row

Finally, many sketches for the Rondo suggest that on some level Berg associated the character Alwa with Tristan in Wagner's opera. The most obvious similarities between the two are the familial relationship between Alwa and Dr. Schön and Alwa's idealized love for Lulu. In his sketches, Berg specifies that Alwa, like Tristan, is to be a Heldentenor, to which he adds "Tristan."[10] And there are numerous sketches of the Tristan chord, which occurs in the climax of the Rondo (mm. 335–36) as Alwa sings, "Mignon, I love you."[11]

Although Berg composed the Rondo only one or two years after the Sonata (parts may have been written simultaneously), his twelve-tone techniques are markedly different. My comments in the discussion that follows are based on isolated sketches in which Berg illustrates these techniques, and on compositional sketches, many of which show order numbers and row forms for highly complex passages.

In row and compositional sketches that Berg wrote on Alwa's row chart (cited briefly in my discussion of formats), Berg attempts in various ways to expand his method of twelve-tone composing and perhaps to connect his earlier and later styles. As shown in Figure 44, Berg derives subsidiary rows from Alwa's row by many of the same operations he had applied to the source row in 1927. For instance, on staff 11, Berg forms three-note chords by stacking order numbers 1–3, 4–6, 7–9, and 10–12; this procedure is similar to the one through which he derived the Bild Harmonien in 1927. To the far right of staff 1 he extracts the Erdgeist fourths and expresses the remaining pitches as two-note chords; this procedure is analogous to the one used in the following subsidiary row from his row chart of 1927 (Example 44). A particularly interesting row derivation appears on staff 3, where Berg divides contiguous notes of the row among three voices. These voices then become segments of a new row

EXAMPLE 45. Derivation of "Alwa Chromatic" row form

EXAMPLE 46. Schigolch's row

EXAMPLE 47. Derivation of Alwa's theme

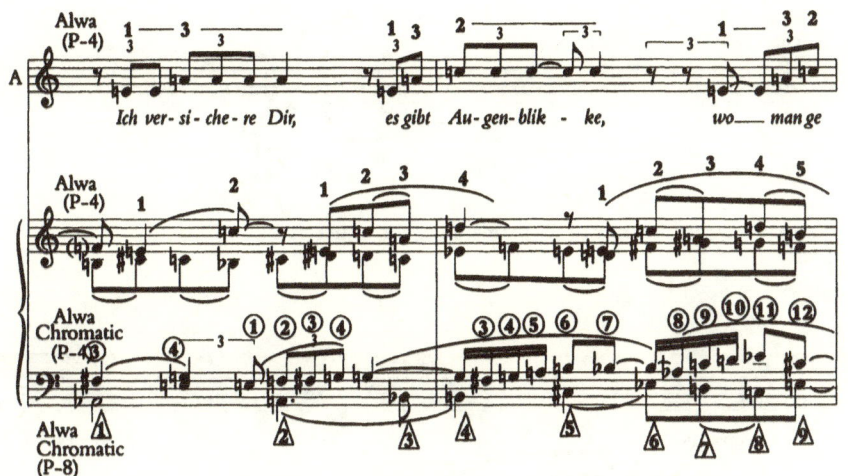

EXAMPLE 48. Analysis of Act II, scene 1, mm. 281–82

(Example 45). Although this latter technique of derivation is completely different from that used to form Schigolch's row, it nonetheless causes the pitch content of the three segments of the row to be identical—moreover, in two of the segments the ordering of pitches is identical. Notice, however, that the segments themselves do not occur in the same order (see Examples 45 and 46). Unfortunately, in his sketch Berg does not justify the similarities between the two rows dramatically. Rather, he simply adds the vague annotation "Verwandtschaft mit Schigolch" (relationship with Schigolch).

Berg's attempt to unify different row forms extends to their compositional expression as well. For instance, on staff 7 (Figure 44), Berg reorders Alwa's row to create two sixths and a "mordent," as he terms it (Example 47). This mordent has the same structure as the second segment of the row just discussed (see Example 45). This figure appears not only within the C_I theme but also as an independent segment, separated from the remaining pitches of Alwa's subsidiary row. In mm. 281–82 (Example 48) the segment is transposed to form a sequence, excluding the other pitches of the row. This sequence moves in parallel motion with the bass line, which is formed by Alwa Chromatic (P_8).

A second method by which Berg associates different rows compositionally is to reorder a row to mimic themes originally expressed by

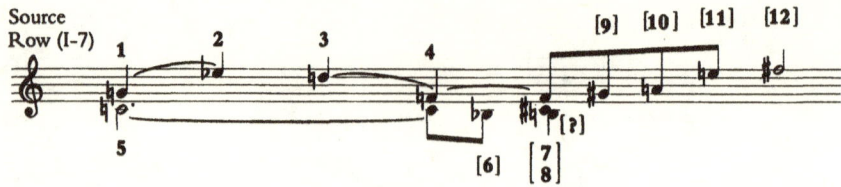

EXAMPLE 49. Variant of C_1 theme using the source row

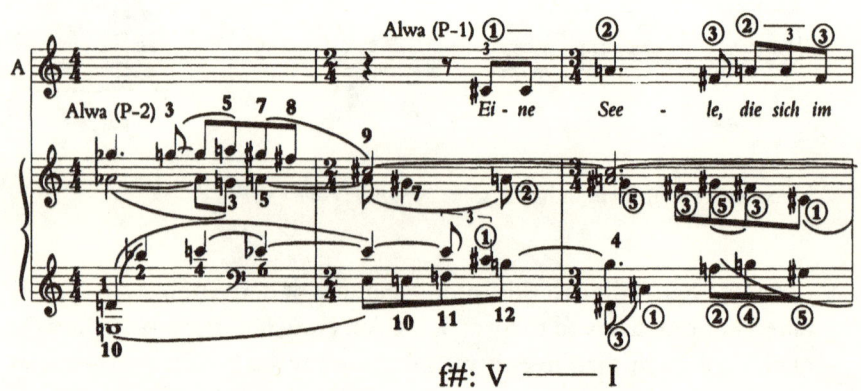

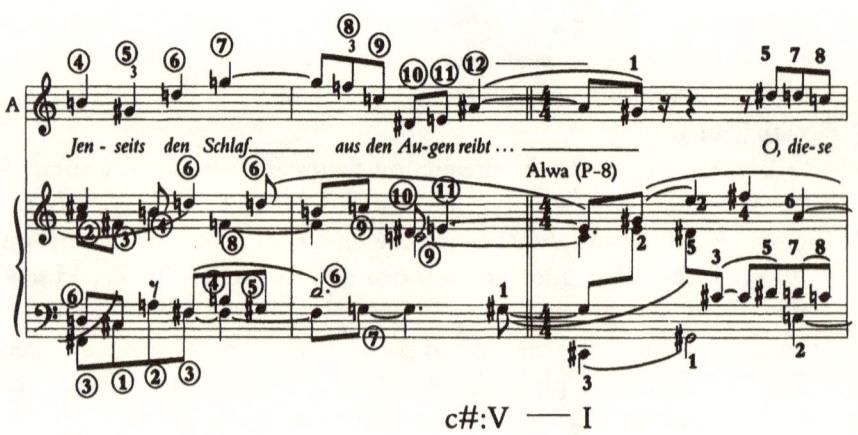

EXAMPLE 50. Analysis of Act II, scene 1, mm. 318–23

152   Why Is Berg's Music Difficult to Analyze?

EXAMPLE 51. Extension of inner voice with Alwa P₁

Alwa's row. (This technique and those following are not restricted to the Rondo; in fact we have observed most of them in compositional sketches dating from 1928.) Compare, for instance, the C₁ theme using Alwa's row (Example 47) with the variant of it that follows using the source row (Example 49).

In many instances, Berg reorders rows to articulate tonal harmonic progressions. In the coda of the Sonata, he "frames" the introduction (mm. 615–16) with the clearly audible harmonies of D-flat major and E major—the E major functioning as a dominant seventh chord in third inversion to the following A-minor chord. In the Rondo, Berg uses reordering to create a similar effect (see Example 50). At the coda, he does not simply begin with the dramatic "Eine Seele" theme; rather, he prepares it with a two-measure introduction. At the end of this introduction he merges two row forms, Alwa P₂ and Alwa P₁, to form a C-sharp major chord. This C-sharp major chord then functions as a dominant to the following F-sharp minor chord. (Such progressions obviously affect Berg's choice of transposition levels as well.) To acquire the G sharp for this dominant, Berg uses his technique of restating an ordered segment of the row as a melodic fragment. Thus, he takes the G, A, G sharp of the upper line (m. 318) and restates it in mm. 318–19 as an inner voice. Berg extends this inner voice using the row form Alwa P₁ to elaborate the outer voice (Example 51). Notice that the G sharp, F sharp, C sharp of the upper voice of mm. 318–19 is formed by Alwa P₂; the G sharp, F sharp, C sharp of the inner voice is formed by Alwa P₁.

By measure 323, the end of the first line of text, we have "modulated" to C-sharp minor. Berg does not articulate the arrival on the tonic to the degree that he does in m. 320, but this treatment seems appropriate since that arrival is not the beginning of a discrete section. Notice, however, that Berg moves from order number 1 (G sharp) to order number 3 (C sharp) to again suggest a dominant-to-tonic tonal progression. In the vocal line, the A sharp, order number 12 (Alwa P_I), functions as a suspension to the following G sharp, a member of this tonic chord. This descending second motive recalls the second segment of the Alwa Chromatic and is used extensively throughout this passage.

Let me now summarize some of the compositional techniques of the Rondo as revealed through Berg's sketches. An important recurring idea in my analysis has been Berg's conscious attempt to extend his twelve-tone method and to unify his earlier and later compositional styles. His most novel attempt at this unification is his derivation of tertiary rows using earlier methods of derivation, as well as the reorderings of Alwa's row to duplicate isolated segments from these tertiary rows. In addition, I have shown how Berg structures the Rondo so that the coda (the final section) culminates earlier sections. Berg achieves this culmination by varying the amount of tonal allusion, by his large-scale completion of themes, by interrupting the form, and by the type of vocal delivery. And finally, I have identified specific features of Berg's dramatic symbolism, for instance, the meaning of the themes in the Rondo, the articulation of conflict between Alwa and Dr. Schön, and the similarity between Alwa and Tristan.

My final analysis comes from the Variations on Wedekind's "Lautenlied," which make up the predominant form of the third act. The tune of the Variations—the song of a prostitute defending her station in life—appears in Act III, scene 1, in connection with Lulu and the Marquis, and as the basis of a rather grandiose set of variations in the interlude between scenes 1 and 2 of Act III. In addition, the Variations are interspersed throughout the final scene. Berg's sketches reveal his wry humor, for the Variations represent Lulu's clients, each of whom is but a variation or version of the other.

I have already noted the overall dramatic and musical function of the Variations: Berg's "turned-around Bolero" (as he called it) forms a transition from the "false glitter" of Act III, scene 1, to the poverty of Act III, scene 2. This transition is articulated through a gradual dissolution of tonality: the first variation is tonal; the second variation, polytonal; the third variation, atonal; and the fourth variation, twelve-tone.

Both Perle and Jarman have made many insightful comments about the Variations. Jarman describes the gradual absorption of the theme into a twelve-tone context, which he correctly likens to the absorption of Dr. Schön's row into the source row that occurs in the unfolding at Schön's death scene. He also identifies the rows with which Berg expresses various segments of the Wedekind tune.[12] Perle too emphasizes an organic relationship between variations that extends beyond the simple inclusion of the Wedekind tune. For him the Variations demonstrate a gradual emergence or development of twelve-tone composition. Thus, even in earlier variations he finds segments that suggest Berg's use of the twelve-tone method. For instance, he describes the chromatic bass line of Variation 2 as "suggestive of Schigolch's Serial Trope," and he describes Variation 3 (which Berg heads as atonal) as "derived very freely from Alwa's series."[13]

For my own analysis, I was initially drawn to Variation 4, which Berg lavishly analyzed in his *Particell*. With the meticulousness usually reserved for compositional sketches of especially complex passages, Berg indicates order numbers for the entire variation, differentiating row forms with colored pencil and circled order numbers (Figure 45).

Yet the twelve-tone method he uses here is far less complicated than that in the Duet; at least one author has already analyzed it without Berg's assistance.[14] Rather than examine the details of Berg's twelve-tone technique in this variation, then, I want to focus on a more fundamental but as yet undiscussed property of the entire set of variations that is less accessible from the printed score.

The first sketch that alludes to this property, Figure 46, shows Berg in the midst of an all-out battle. The frenzied nature of the sketch recalls Berg's most circuitous sketches of multiple roles—and indeed he is again struggling with the same problem of establishing and coordinating many parameters simultaneously.

Although the sketch is headed with "Zwischenspiel III 1/2" (Interlude III 1/2), it is actually a compositional sketch of the Procurer's aria in Act III, scene 1 (the first appearance of the Wedekind theme), which Berg has simply overlaid with ideas for the Variations. For instance, the margins of the sketch reveal a number of tonal schemes through which Berg could make the transition from the C major of the first variation to the key of the theme in the opening of Act III, scene 2. At the same time, he is

FIGURE 45. Berg's analysis of the twelve-tone variation in the *Particell* (mm. 730–31). ÖNB Musiksammlung F 21 Berg 29/III, fol. 47r

FIGURE 46. Sketch of the Variations (Act III, scenes 1 and 2), overlaid on a sketch of the Procurer's aria. ÖNB Musiksammlung F 21 Berg XLIII, fol. 111r

determining the sequence and compositional style of each variation, for instance, that one of the variations would be polytonal and that it would appear immediately after the tonal variation. At this point, the only fixed parameter appears to be the metric plan; according to both the heading in the upper margin and the two lower sketches in the right-hand margin, Berg is constructing a symmetrical plan of triple, quadruple, quintuple, quadruple, triple meter—thus reinforcing the palindromic idea of the opera.

In the right-hand margin of the lower diagram, Berg assigns a letter to each variation: the initial 3/4 variation is a; the 4/4 variation, b; the 5/4, e; the returning 4/4, f; and the final 3/4, g. On the sketch one can see where Berg repeatedly superimposes this metric plan onto the Wedekind theme. Since the theme is in triple meter, the measure numbers indicate the initial 3/4 division. When the theme repeats, however, Berg places brackets on the sketch to show its immediate division into 4/4 and subsequent metric displacement. Similarly, with the third repetition of the theme, Berg moves directly from 4/4 to 5/4, and the 5e brackets superimposed on the sketch indicate this new division. Berg differentiates the next meter, 4/4, from the original 4/4 with his label 4f; the last variation, in 3/4, is notated with brackets in the music.

Why was the metric accent of these various meters upon the Wedekind tune of such burning concern to Berg? While the answer to this question is certainly present in this sketch, it becomes far more apparent in later sketches where Berg adopted a less convoluted or confusing format.

Figure 47 is one of four such sketches. Rather than superimpose all the meters upon a single melodic line, Berg has created a chart in which each meter is displayed separately. By comparing each meter with the Wedekind tune that appears above it, one can see the beat of the original 3/4 division on which each pattern begins. For instance, the 4/4 meter of the second variation begins after the pickup of the 3/4 version (marked by dark bar lines in Berg's sketch). The 4/4 division also ends on the pickup; thus the 5/4 meter begins at the same time as the 4/4 did (staff 3). The many dots between slashes suggest that Berg has carefully counted out the beats of each division, just as he counted notes in his sketches for extraction type rows. In fact, although the row sketches deal with pitch and our present sketches focus on meter, the issue is exactly

FIGURE 47. Metric chart of the Variations (Act III, scenes 1 and 2). ÖNB Musiksammlung F 21 Berg 28/IX, fol. 1r

the same: Berg is searching for numeric patterns that create circularity. In his twelve-tone rows, circularity consisted of patterns of extraction that would allow him to generate twelve pitches without "breaks," or shifts to adjacent notes. Here it consists of metric patterns that allow him to state the beginning of the theme in the opening of the final scene as an upbeat—that is, without metric displacement. As we see in Figure 47, he eventually had to abandon his ideal of a metric palindrome to achieve this. On staff 4 Berg superimposes a seven-beat, rather than a four-beat, metric pattern for the twelve-tone variation (marked with brackets). Its last beat forms the upbeat to the theme, allowing the triple division of the theme—the opening of the final scene—to begin on a strong beat.

I have demonstrated in earlier analyses how Berg manipulates his twelve-tone technique to articulate the structure of the text, to express dramatic symbolism, and to suggest tonality. However, in his Variations the restrictions may be too great, for I must confess that I find them less aesthetically satisfying than many other passages of the opera. It is largely Berg's mastery of orchestration that redeems them, but that is a topic for another book.

Concluding Remarks

> One of the things I find most useful about sketches is that they give you the simple possibility of seeing something that the composer rejected.[1]
>
> Joseph Kerman
>
> I've never been able to persuade myself that I knew more about the work, from an analytical point of view, after I studied the sketches than I did before I began.[2]
>
> Douglas Johnson

While the comments that serve as epigraphs to these remarks focus on the study of Beethoven's sketches—not Berg's—they nonetheless typify many scholars' attitudes toward sketch study in general. One of the reasons sketches clarify analysis in this study is that the sketches—however preliminary or fragmentary—are retained in the final version. This is a fortuitous outcome of Berg's compositional process; as I demonstrated in Chapter 1, Berg's sketches feature the gradual *addition* of musical or dramatic parameters to an initial idea, rather than the rejection of that idea. Berg's compositional process was a result of the complexity of his music, for instead of assembling many musical and dramatic parameters simultaneously, he chose to implement them systematically, one by one.

To make the theoretical discoveries presented in this book, I have entered the realm of what is generally considered historical musicology, determining the chronology of the sketches as far as is presently possible, defining the formats of the sketches, and outlining Berg's compositional process. One can, for instance, immediately see the importance of chronology in identifying a discovery, as I did in Chapter 5. One can see its importance in understanding the correct evolution of a composer's style, as I demonstrated in Chapter 6. But it is also useful for more subtle reasons as in Chapter 3, where I arranged sketches of multiple roles chronologically to determine Berg's techniques of associating characters. Thus, by utilizing chronology and compositional process in my analyses, I have joined the traditions of theory and musicology in a meaningful way.

Kerman has termed the analysis featured in this study "descriptive analysis"; that is, it codifies or clarifies the musical language of the composer.[3] Given the antianalytical tone of the word "descriptive," I would prefer the term "organic." By this, I mean my analytical conclusions arise from structures already present in the music, rather than from analytical systems applied to the music. These conclusions can, of course, then be applied to other areas of the opera, for often theoretical principles featured in a single sketch can be a governing feature of the entire work— or even other works written during the same period. Anthony Pople, for instance, discusses a sketch for the *Violin Concerto* in which Berg labels segments of the row according to the harmonic successions they imply —a procedure he also uses in *Lulu,* although less systematically.[4]

And finally, let me comment on the interaction of sketches with the final version. Too often these elements are treated as discrete: we analyze music to learn about the piece but study sketches to learn how the composer worked. In reality, however, they should form a dialogue: the music should augment the ideas we see in sketches, and the sketches should provide insights that we may not see or understand in the music. Sketches show processes that are present but perhaps obscure in the finished score. When we make use of sketches, it is as if we were somehow able to X-ray the music, or peel back its layers to see its inner workings; through this process we arrive at a more precise view of Berg's twelve-tone language.

Discussing Cerha's orchestration of Act III of *Lulu,* Perle remarks: "Our first and most important obligation to Berg's artistic legacy is achieved—the rescue, for ourselves and posterity, of his *chef d'oeuvre* and one of the supreme masterpieces of its genre in the entire repertory, through its restoration, in every most essential respect, to the composer's own conception."[5] Perle stresses the necessity of restoring *Lulu* "in every most essential respect, to the composer's own conception." We owe this same degree of precision and individuality to analyses and discussions of the opera. Berg's sketches give us valuable insights—into his creative procedures, the evolution of his style, his hidden extramusical devices, and the organization of his music. And our knowledge will undoubtedly increase as more letters and documentary evidence become available.

Notes

Introduction

1. Theodor Adorno, *Berg: Der Meister des kleinsten Übergangs* (Vienna, 1968), p. 129. I would like to thank Lee Rothfarb for the translation.
2. Willi Reich, "Alban Berg's *Lulu*," *Musical Quarterly* 22 (1936): 383–401.
3. Willi Reich, *The Life and Work of Alban Berg*, trans. Cornelius Cardew (London, 1965), pp. 7–8.
4. George Perle, "The Music of *Lulu*: A New Analysis," *Journal of the American Musicological Society* 12 (1959): 185–200.
5. Perle, "*Lulu*: A New Analysis," p. 189.
6. Perle, "*Lulu*: A New Analysis," pp. 187–88.
7. Perle, *The Operas of Alban Berg*, vol. 2: "*Lulu*" (Berkeley and Los Angeles, 1985).
8. Rosemary Hilmar, *Alban Berg, 1885–1935: Katalog zur Ausstellung der Österreichischen Nationalbibliothek* (Vienna, 1985), p. 203.
9. Reich consistently cited Berg's row charts as proof of the relation between the subsidiary rows and the source row. Perle, in fact, was searching for evidence of this relation in the actual music of *Lulu*.
10. Perle, "The Film Interlude of *Lulu*," *International Alban Berg Society Newsletter* 11 (Spring 1982): 3–8, and *Operas*, vol. 2: "*Lulu*," p. 63.
11. Douglas Jarman, "*Lulu*: The Sketches," *International Alban Berg Society Newsletter* 6 (June 1978): 7–8.
12. Perle, *Operas*, vol. 2: "*Lulu*," p. 270.
13. Jarman, "*Lulu*: The Sketches," pp. 4–8.
14. Douglas Jarman, *The Music of Alban Berg* (Berkeley and Los Angeles, 1979).
15. Douglas Johnson, "Beethoven Scholars and Beethoven's Sketches," *Nineteenth-Century Music* 2 (1978): 3–17.
16. Carl Schachter, "Beethoven's Sketches for the First Movement of Op. 14, No. 1: A Study in Design," *Journal of Music Theory* 26, no. 1 (1982): 1–21.
17. Schachter, "Beethoven's Sketches," p. 18.
18. This sketch is reproduced in Hans Jancik, ed., *Hugo Wolf, Sämtliche Werke*, Band 19, no. 1, *Fragmente und Skizzen* (Vienna, 1992), p. 305; however, it is identified as part of a sketch for "Der Schreckenberger" (pp. x and 347).
19. For a detailed study of this process, see Hans Eppstein, "Zu Hugo Wolfs Liedskizzen," *Österreichische Musikzeitschrift* 39 (1984): 645–56; and Susan Youens, "The Song Sketches of Hugo Wolf," *Current Musicology* 44 (1990): 5–37.

20. Eppstein argues that in Wolf's lieder "the vocal line and piano accompaniment essentially originated as a unit" ("Zu Hugo Wolfs Liedskizzen," p. 655).
21. Sieghard Brandenburg, "On Beethoven Scholars and Beethoven's Sketches," *Nineteenth-Century Music* 2 (1979): 271.
22. Lewis Lockwood, "The Autograph of the First Movement of Beethoven's Sonata for Violoncello and Pianoforte, Opus 69," in *The Music Forum*, vol. 2, ed. William Mitchell and Felix Salzer (New York, 1970), p. 90.

Chapter 1

1. The Alban Berg Nachlass contains the musical and literary effects in Helene Berg's possession at the time of Berg's death. The remaining few autograph sources for *Lulu* are in the following libraries: Wiener Stadt- und Landesbibliothek, the British Library, the Bayerische Staatsbibliothek, and the Paul Sacher Archive.
2. See Rosemary Hilmar, *Katalog der Musikhandschriften, Schriften und Studien Alban Bergs im Fond Alban Berg und der weiteren handschriftlichen Quellen im Besitz der Österreichischen Nationalbibliothek*, Alban Berg Studien, Band 1 (Vienna, 1980), items 35–95, 96–100, 378–82, 392–95, 437.
3. The sketches probably arrived at the Nationalbibliothek in this condition. Thus, Berg may have arranged them in this order.
4. Berg reports to Webern in a letter dated May 6, 1934, that although he has finished composing *Lulu*, he must now "overhaul" it from the beginning. Much of this overhaul may have consisted of retouches of the *Particell*.
5. Und da ich beim Fragen bin, zum Schluss noch etwas, was mir ausserordentlich am Herzen liegt: Sie sprachen seinerzeit davon, die ganze *Lulu* solle aus *einer* Zwölftonreihe entwickelt werden. Aus der Analyse Reichs scheint mir nun aber hervorzugehen, dass zumindest die Pariser Szene nicht als Zwölftonstück d u r c h -komponiert ist. Das bedeutet also, dass Sie in einem zentralen Punkt vom Zwölftonprinzip abgegangen sind und es bedarf keiner Erläuterung, was das prinzipiell heisst. Wollen Sie mir sagen, wie es damit sich verhält? Bitte nur eine Karte, ich möchte Ihnen um keinen Preis Ihre Zeit stehlen, die weiss Gott zu wichtigerem da ist. ÖNB Musiksammlung F 21 Berg 1535/60.
6. Die von Ihnen angedeutete Struktur der Variationen war mir aus Reichs Analyse bekannt; was mich am meisten bedrängt ist die Frage ob *sonst* das ganze in Zwölftontechnik geschrieben ist (wie es ja ursprünglich die Absicht war); oder ob Sie wieder, und gewiss mit den denkbar schwerwiegendsten Gründen, sich "unprinzipiell" verhalten haben. ÖNB Musiksammlung F 21 Berg 1535/61.
7. The term I use here, "format," is from Martha Hyde's article "The Format and Function of Schoenberg's Twelve-Tone Sketches," *Journal of the American Musicological Society* 36 (1983): 453–80. My methodology in the following discussion is based on hers.
8. Hyde, "Format and Function," p. 454.
9. Conversely, some of these compositional sketches may have been added later.
10. See the sketches ÖNB Musiksammlung F 28/VII, fol. 3r–3v, and F 21 Berg 28/III, fol. 25v.
11. Ernst Hilmar, "Die verschiedenen Entwicklungsstadien in den Kompositionsskizzen," in *50 Jahre Wozzeck von Alban Berg*, ed. Otto Kolleritsch (Graz, 1978), p. 24.
12. I am aware, of course, that a musical idea may be a component of the work's structure even though it is not featured in a sketch.
13. Berg's copies of *Erdgeist* and *Pandora's Box* contain many annotations indicating the syllabic stress of the spoken text.

14. According to Berg's letter to Webern of May 6, 1934, he would only be able to begin the orchestration by June 1934. See Willi Reich, *The Life and Work of Alban Berg,* trans. Cornelius Cardew (London, 1965), p. 93.

Chapter 2

1. It is unclear who mixed these sketches together. It may, in fact, have been Berg.

2. For instance, Berg would experiment far in advance with large-scale plans for later sections—sometimes even completing their principal musical themes.

3. Rosemary Hilmar, *Katalog der Musikhandschriften, Schriften und Studien Alban Bergs im Fond Alban Berg und der weiteren handschriftlichen Quellen im Besitz der Österreichischen Nationalbibliothek,* Alban Berg Studien, Band 1 (Vienna, 1980), pp. 32 and 27.

4. While drafts of letters are usually reliable forms of evidence, it is nonetheless possible that Berg occasionally wrote them on old sketches. Thus, these drafts need to be evaluated in conjunction with other evidence.

5. Berg also used twelve-staff paper in sketches dating from 1933–34.

6. These early sketches also tend to be much more colorfully annotated; that is, Berg sometimes used four shades of colored pencil on a single sketch.

7. Changes in handwriting and address stamps are other external evidence; however, I rarely include them in my discussion. After a careful study of Berg's handwriting during the seven years he composed *Lulu,* I have been unable to discern any consistent changes that one could use for dating purposes. And while Berg does occasionally use address stamps, I have found them minimally helpful.

8. See, for instance, Willi Reich, *The Life and Work of Alban Berg,* trans. Cornelius Cardew (London, 1965), p. 42.

9. Lieber Doktor, Ich habe beschlossen im kommenden Früsommer mit der Komposition einer Oper zu beginnen. Hierzu habe ich 2 Pläne von denen *einer ganz bestimmt* ausgeführt wird. Es fragt sich also nur *welcher.* Zu diesem Zweck frage ich auch Sie um Rat: Es ist: entweder *Und Pippa Tanzt* oder *Lulu* (Letzteres durch zusammenziehung von *Erdgeist* u[nd] *Büchse der Pandora* zu einem 3 aktigen (6–7 bildrigen) Opernbuch). Was sagen Sie dazu? Da ich unbedingt eins davon (oder ev[entuell] beide) komponieren werde ist also eine Entscheidung *welches* von beiden (resp[ectiv] ev[entuell] welches zuerst) vonnöten. Theodor Adorno, *Berg: Der Meister des kleinsten Übergangs* (Vienna, 1968), pp. 32–33.

10. Das Wachsen Ihrer Opernpläne verfolge ich natürlich mit grössten Spannung; *Leonce und Lena* schiene mir ausserordentlich geeignet; es ist nur von Julius Weissman komponiert, d.h. also gar nicht. Aber *Lulu* wäre natürlich auch sehr gut und wenn Sie sich zur *Pippa* entschliessen, so genügt der Entschluss, um Hauptmann zu erretten. ÖNB Musiksammlung F 21 Berg 1535/34.

11. Juliane Brand, Christopher Hailey, and Donald Harris, eds., *The Berg-Schoenberg Correspondence: Selected Letters* (New York, 1987), p. 369.

12. See Berg's letter to Josef Polnauer of August 28, 1928. Handschriftensammlung, Wiener Stadt- und Landesbibliothek I.N. 184.056.

13. ÖNB Musiksammlung F 21 Berg 28/L. Each leaf is formed from four pieces of music paper that have been glued together.

14. Mosco Carner, *Alban Berg: The Man and the Work* (London, 1975), pp. 60–61.

15. ÖNB Musiksammlung F21 Berg 80/II, fol. 1r–1v, and F 21 Berg 28/XL, fol. 6r; F 21 Berg 28/XXIII, fol. 2r.

16. Douglass Green discusses this sketch in detail in "A False Start for *Lulu:* An Early Version of the Prologue," in *Alban Berg: Historical and Analytical Perspectives,* ed. David

Gable and Robert Morgan (Oxford, 1991), pp. 203–213. See also Thomas F. Ertelt's excellent article " 'Hereinspaziert . . .' Ein Früher Entwurf des Prologs zu Alban Bergs *Lulu*," *Österreichische Musikzeitschrift* 41 (1986): 15–25.

17. See Berg's letter to Helene Berg of June 17, 1928. Alban Berg, *Letters to His Wife*, trans. Bernard Grun (New York, 1971), p. 362.

18. For a discussion of the possible origins of Berg's number of fate, see Douglas Jarman, *The Music of Alban Berg* (Berkeley and Los Angeles, 1979), pp. 228–30.

19. ÖNB Musiksammlung F 21 Berg 28/XV–XVI.

20. See Brand, Hailey, and Harris, eds., *Berg-Schoenberg Correspondence*, p. 373. I discuss this letter in more detail in Chapter 5.

21. Adorno inquires about Berg's progress on his opera in a letter dated August 17, 1928 (ÖNB Musiksammlung F 21 Berg 1535/36). When Berg's response to this letter becomes accessible, it may reveal how much of the opera Berg had completed by this time.

22. This source also contains two leaves of a later section of the opera.

23. ÖNB Musiksammlung F 21 Berg 80/V, fols. 18r–34v. The content, paper type, sketching technique, and writing implements suggest that this notebook dates from 1928. In addition, it bears an address stamp that Berg used in his correspondence throughout that year. F 21 Berg 80/V, fols. 1r–17v and 37r–39v, is actually a separate notebook. It uses fourteen-staff paper and most probably dates from 1930.

24. These are the same shades of colored pencil with which Berg embellished his row chart from 1927 and the corresponding smaller row charts F 21 Berg XL, fol. 6r, and F 21 Berg 80/II, fol. 1r–1v.

25. This hypothesis is also supported by Berg's letter to Schoenberg of August 6, 1931, in which he comments, "The principal difficulty remains shaping the text, finalization of which goes hand in hand with composing, indeed the text often has to be directly fitted into the music." Brand, Hailey, and Harris, eds., *Berg-Schoenberg Correspondence*, p. 414.

26. I quote an excerpt from this letter in Chapter 3. F 21 Berg 80/VI, fol. 9r, appears to have "Aug[ust] 1928" written in its upper left-hand corner. This evidence does not appear on the microfilm of the sketch because the corner is folded over.

27. Brand, Hailey, and Harris, eds., *Berg-Schoenberg Correspondence*, p. 387.

28. Brand, Hailey, and Harris, eds., *Berg-Schoenberg Correspondence*, p. 388.

29. Deine Entdeckungen auf dem Gebiete der "Reihen"-Konstruktion schienen mir von grosser Bedeutung, denn die Möglichkeit, aus der "Urreihe" durch *Permutation* (ich glaube, dass man auf mathematischen Gebiete diese Art der Ableitung, wie Du sie vorgenommen hast, so nennt) Reihen zu gewinnen, die zwar neu sind aber doch in *ursächlichem* Zusammenhange mit jener (der Urreihe) stehn, also die Möglichkeit, für den Fall (wie er offenbar bei Dir jetzt eingetreten ist), als man mit vier Grundformen und deren Transpositionen nicht auszukommen vermag, statt neue Reihen *erfinden* zu müssen —solche durch *Ableitung* gewinnen zu können, erscheint mir für den "Zusammenhang" von weitgehendstem Nutzen; ja vielleicht ist das überhaupt die günstigste Lösung dieses Problems.

30. The following are sketches of cyclic row derivation: F 21 Berg 28/X, fol. 1r–1v; 28/XI, fol. 1r–1v; 28/XX, fols. 4r–5r; 28/XXIII, fol. 3r–3v; 28/XXX, fols. 4v and 16r; 28/XL, fol. 7r. The following are sketches of *Der Wein* and therefore also date from 1929: F 21 Berg 28/XXX, fols. 1r–2r and 4r; 80/II, fols. 2v–9r; 80/VI, fol. 8r–8v; 80/VIII, fols. 9r–9v and 12r–12v.

31. ÖNB Musiksammlung F 21 Berg 80/II, fols. 12r–35v. Berg appears to have used this booklet again for the orchestration of *Lulu* (1934–35).

32. ÖNB Musiksammlung F 21 Berg 28/XXIV, fols. 22v–23r. As I have noted, Berg wrote part of this draft in 1928. It is probably impossible to distinguish the division

(assuming one exists) between the sketches he wrote in 1928 and those he wrote in 1929.

33. Ich habe — nach 10monatiger Pause — hier gleich an der *Lulu* zu arbeiten begonnen, und bin ziemlich rasch in Schwung gekommen. Ernst Hilmar, "Alban Bergs Selbstzeugnisse zu Entstehung und Aufführbarkeit der Oper *Lulu*," in Alban Berg, *"Lied der Lulu": Faksimile-Ausgabe der Anton V. Webern gewidmeten autographen Partitur* (Vienna, 1985), p. 13.

34. The other sketches on this double leaf undoubtedly also date from 1929. ÖNB Musiksammlung F 21 Berg 28/XXVIII, fols. 1r–2v.

35. ÖNB Musiksammlung F 21 Berg 432/26.

36. Hilmar, *Katalog der Musikhandschriften, Schriften und Studien Alban Bergs*, pp. 29–30.

37. The completed double acrostic is shown in Erich Alban Berg, ed., *Alban Berg: Leben und Werk in Daten und Bildern* (Frankfurt, 1976), p. 216.

38. See also Alma Mahler, *Mein Leben* (Berlin, 1960), p. 181. In her entry "Wien, 1930," she comments on her daughter's engagement and marriage.

39. Erich Alban Berg, ed., *Alban Berg*, p. 208.

40. See note 33.

41. Brand, Hailey, and Harris, eds., *Berg-Schoenberg Correspondence*, p. 405.

42. Brand, Hailey, and Harris, eds., *Berg-Schoenberg Correspondence*, p. 414.

43. Ernst Hilmar, "Alban Bergs Selbstzeugnisse," p. 14.

44. See note 23.

45. ÖNB Musiksammlung F 21 Berg 432/27.

46. ÖNB Musiksammlung F 21 Berg 1309/82–83.

47. Brand, Hailey, and Harris, eds., *Berg-Schoenberg Correspondence*, pp. 421–22.

48. ÖNB Musiksammlung F 21 Berg 432/28 and F 21 Berg 1473/262–64. Berg also worked on *Lulu* during the winter at a spa hotel in Hofgastein. In a letter to Schoenberg, February 16, 1932, he notes that composition has not gone well, but he has made progress with the "text and musical disposition." Brand, Hailey, and Harris, eds., *Berg-Schoenberg Correspondence*, p. 431.

49. Brand, Hailey, and Harris, eds., *Berg-Schoenberg Correspondence*, p. 433.

50. ÖNB Musiksammlung F 21 Berg 28/XXXVII, fol. 36v.

51. Ernst Hilmar, "Alban Bergs Selbstzeugnisse," p. 15.

52. Hilmar, "Alban Bergs Selbstzeugnisse," p. 15.

53. ich steck' immer noch im II. Akt: eine schwere Geburt, aber ich glaube, jetzt, wo ich ihn wesentlich umgearbeitet habe, am richtigen Weg zu sein. Hilmar, "Alban Bergs Selbstzeugnisse," p. 15.

54. Seit ein Paar Tagen wills bei mir nicht recht gehn. Bis dahin aber gings ganz gut: ich habe endlich, endlich den II. Akt beendet. Hilmar, "Alban Bergs Selbstzeugnisse," p. 15.

55. Seit ich *hier* bin, kann ich die Angst nicht los werden, dass auch hier die Nazi siegen werden, bezw. unsere Regierung nicht stark genug sein *kann*, es zu verhindern.

56. Brand, Hailey, and Harris, eds., *Berg-Schoenberg Correspondence*, p. 449.

57. Soll ich noch deutlicher werden und Ihnen verrathen, dass wir aus diesen Gründen hier bleiben, wo wir eben viel billiger leben kann als in Wien; dass es aber kein Vergnügen ist, in dieser Saukälte, eingeschlossen von Eis und Schnee, — bei einfachen Fenstern, ohne Wasserleitung . . durchzuhalten. Musikhandschriftensammlung, Wiener Stadt- und Landesbibliothek MH 14261/c.

58. ÖNB Musiksammlung F 21 Berg 1300/7. The letter that elicited Berg's draft is dated December 14, 1933. That the draft is written on sketches from the end of Act III, scene 1, suggests that Berg wrote the final scene in 1934. Autograph sources dating from this last period include the following: F 21 Berg 28/V: 1933/34; 28/VI: 1933/34 (excluding fols. 7r–12r); 28/IX: 1933/34; 28/X, fol. 3r–3v: 1934; 28/XII: 1933/34; 28/XX, fol. 6r–6v: 1934; 28/XXV: 1934; 28/XL, fols. 1v–5v: 1934 and fols. 9r–10v: 1933;

28/XLI–XLII: 1933; 28/XLIII–XLIV: 1933/34; 28/XLV: 1933; 28/XLVI: 1933/34; 28/XLVII–XLVIII: 1934; 28/XLIX: 1933/34; 80/IV: mostly 1934; 80/VI: 1934, except fol. 8r–8v; 80/VII, fol. 2r–2v: 1933; 80/VIII, fols. 14r–16v: 1934; 80/IX: 1934/35.

59. Ernst Hilmar, "Alban Bergs Selbstzeugnisse," p. 16.
60. Berg, *Letters to His Wife*, p. 421.
61. Berg, *Letters to His Wife*, p. 424.
62. Ernst Hilmar, "Alban Bergs Selbstzeugnisse," p. 17.
63. Hilmar, "Alban Bergs Selbstzeugnisse," p. 17.
64. Rosemary Hilmar, *Katalog der Musikhandschriften, Schriften und Studien Alban Bergs*, p. 35.
65. ÖNB Musiksammlung F 21 Berg 28/VIII.
66. See, for instance, Erich Alban Berg, *Der unverbesserliche Romantiker: Alban Berg, 1885–1935* (Vienna, 1985), pp. 115–17.
67. George Perle, *The Operas of Alban Berg*, vol. 2: *"Lulu"* (Berkeley and Los Angeles, 1985), p. 269. For a detailed discussion of the work involved in completing the third act, see pp. 269–80; see also Friedrich Cerha, *Arbeitsbericht zur Herstellung des 3. Akts der Oper "Lulu" von Alban Berg* (Vienna, 1979).
68. Letter from Berg to Rudolph Kolisch, dated September 22, 1935. Handschriftensammlung, Wiener Stadt- und Landesbibliothek I.N. 202.981.

Chapter 3

1. Juliane Brand, Christopher Hailey, and Donald Harris, eds., *The Berg-Schoenberg Correspondence: Selected Letters* (New York, 1987), p. 406.
2. Note that in the long quotation in the text above Berg uses the phrase "fall victim to her." Accordingly, I refer to Dr. Goll, the Painter, and Dr. Schön collectively as "the victims," although there can be no doubt that if these men are Lulu's victims, they are equally victims of their own folly.
3. ÖNB Musiksammlung F 21 Berg 28/III, F 21 Berg 28/VI, and F 21 Berg 80/III. Many of the sketches in this booklet are a hybrid of concept sketches, form sketches, and sketches of dramatic symbolism. Thus, rather than attempt to categorize them, I simply describe their content.
4. The booklet has, for instance, a detailed dramatic outline of Act I, scene 1, which Berg would have completed before he began composing that section of the opera in 1928.
5. ÖNB Musiksammlung F 21 Berg 28/III, fol. 39v.
6. ÖNB Musiksammlung F 21 Berg 28/III, fol. 38v.
7. The sketches in this example were written almost concurrently, but it is difficult to affix specific dates; however, chronology—the *ordering* of these sketches—allows us to see the gradual evolution of Berg's ideas on multiple roles.
8. See, for instance, the sketch ÖNB Musiksammlung F 21 Berg 28/III, fol. 38r.
9. See Frank Wedekind, *Erdgeist / Die Büchse der Pandora. Tragödien* (Munich, 1980).
10. George Perle, *The Operas of Alban Berg* vol. 2: *"Lulu"* (Berkeley and Los Angeles, 1985), p. 60. Note, however, that the Painter's double appears immediately after Geschwitz arrives with her completed portrait of Lulu. In the ensuing quartet, Lulu, Geschwitz, Alwa, and Schigolch reminisce at length about the Painter, his relationship with Lulu, and his suicide. I would like to thank Alyson Brown for pointing out this connection.
11. Perle, *Operas*, vol. 2: *"Lulu,"* p. 60.
12. Perle, *Operas*, vol. 2: *"Lulu,"* p. 81.

13. I would like to thank Dr. Otto Biba of the Gesellschaft der Musikfreunde in Vienna for helping me decipher this annotation and for explaining its relation to *Lohengrin*.

14. See Douglas Jarman, "Alban Berg, Wilhelm Fliess, and the Secret Programme of the *Violin Concerto*," *International Alban Berg Society Newsletter* 12 (Fall/Winter 1982): 9.

15. The opening of the variation shows a repeated B in the timpani (m. 101) that mimics the repeated F in the opening of the wedding march. This figure is followed by the F, B flat, B flat of the Marquis's vocal line (m. 101), that is, the initial three pitches of the chorus of the wedding march. Might this be Berg's elusive reference?

16. Perle, *Operas*, vol. 2: "*Lulu*," p. 149.

17. Karl Kraus, "Die Büchse der Pandora," in *Literatur und Lüge* (Munich, 1958), p. 12.

18. Reich, *The Life and Work of Alban Berg*, trans. Cornelius Cardew (London, 1965), p. 156.

19. Reich, *Alban Berg*, p. 156.

20. Und dann die gewaltige Doppeltragödie, deren zweiten Teil Sie heute schauen werden, die Tragödie von der gehetzten, ewig missverstandenen Frauenanmut, der eine armselige Welt bloss in das Prokrustesbett ihrer Moralbegriffe zu steigen erlaubt. Ein Speissrutenlauf der Frau, die vom Schöpferwillen dem Egoismus des Besitzers zu dienen nicht bestimmt ist, die nur in der Freiheit zu ihren höheren Werten emporsteigen kann. Dass die flüchtige Schönheit des Tropenvogels mehr beseligt als der sichere Besitz, bei dem die Enge des Bauers die Pracht des Gefieders verwundet, hat sich noch kein Vogelsteller gesagt. Sei die Hetäre ein Traum des Mannes. Aber die Wirklichkeit soll sie ihm zur Hörigen—Hausfrau oder Maitresse—machen, weil das soziale Ehrbedürfnis ihm selbst über den Traum geht. Kraus, *Literatur und Lüge*, p. 11.

21. Willi Reich, "Alban Berg's *Lulu*," *Musical Quarterly* 22 (1936): 389.

22. Berg writes "Rodrigo Diener Uniform wie früher Diener" (Rodrigo servant uniform like earlier servant) on a sketch where he works out symmetries in action in the film scenario (F 21 Berg 28/X, fol. 4v). Thus, Berg was aware of the symmetrical placement of these characters.

23. In the sketch F 21 Berg 28/VI, fol. 10v, Berg experiments with a cryptic dramatic connection between these characters. He appears to write "die Kalt bleiben" (those who remain unmoved).

24. Kraus, *Literatur und Lüge*, p. 14.

25. Both Perle and Jarman point out the impracticality of this triple role, in that the Police Commissioner appears twenty-seven measures after the Banker's exit in Act III, scene 1. I find it odd, however, that Berg never included alternative plans in his sketches. Moreover, some of the sketches for this triple role were completed after he wrote Act III, scene 1, that is, when he was clearly aware of the short time between the Banker's exit and the Police Commissioner's entrance. I can only conclude that he intended these two roles to be played by the same singer.

26. Perle, *Operas*, vol. 2: "*Lulu*," p. 62.

27. Perle, *Operas*, vol. 2: "*Lulu*," p. 146.

28. The sketch F 21 Berg 28/I, fol. 15v, is revealing in this regard, because it shows Berg working out the symmetries of Act II, scenes 1 and 2, based on the groups of characters present in corresponding sections of these scenes.

29. For a detailed discussion of Berg's Film Music scenario, see Perle, *Operas*, vol. 2: "*Lulu*," pp. 149–57. The second half of the Film Music is a retrograde of the first half.

30. Although scholars use Kraus's phrase "the revenge of the world of men" to describe the last scene of *Lulu*, Kraus was, in fact, referring to the whole of *Pandora's Box* (Act II, scene 2, through Act III, scene 2, of *Lulu*). See Kraus, *Literatur und Lüge*, p. 12; and Reich, *Alban Berg*, pp. 157–58.

Chapter 4

1. Mosco Carner, *Alban Berg: The Man and the Work* (London, 1975), p. 218.
2. Willi Reich, "Alban Berg's *Lulu*," *Musical Quarterly* 22 (1936): 391.
3. George Perle, "The Music of *Lulu*: A New Analysis," *Journal of the American Musicology Society* 12 (1959): 187.
4. Perle, "*Lulu:* A New Analysis," p. 187.
5. Willi Reich, "An der Seite von Alban Berg," *Melos* 27 (1960).
6. Klaus Schweizer, *Die Sonatensatzform im Schaffen Alban Bergs* (Stuttgart, 1970), pp. 189–93.
7. See, for instance, Douglas Jarman's excellent summary in his book *The Music of Alban Berg* (Berkeley and Los Angeles, 1979), pp. 203–4.
8. Carner, *Alban Berg*, p. 219.
9. See, for instance, ÖNB Musiksammlung F 21 Berg 28/XXX, fol. 14r.
10. ÖNB Musiksammlung F 21 Berg 29/I, fol. 65r.
11. Schweizer, *Die Sonatensatzform*, p. 193.
12. George Perle, *The Operas of Alban Berg*, vol. 2: "*Lulu*" (Berkeley and Los Angeles, 1985), p. 159.
13. Jarman, *Music of Alban Berg*, p. 120.
14. Schweizer, *Die Sonatensatzform*, p. 192.
15. Hans F. Redlich, *Alban Berg: Versuch einer Würdigung* (Vienna, 1957), p. 239; and Perle, "*Lulu*: Thematic Material and Pitch Organization," *Music Review* 26 (November 1965): 273.
16. This date is significant because Berg (as his letters from this period demonstrate) was developing methods of row derivation that would assure unity between the source row and the subsidiary row.
17. In a later sketch of the same passage (ÖNB Musiksammlung F 21 Berg 28/XXVI, fol. 6r) Berg indicates once again its hybrid nature. He writes "Ur (+ Schön) Reihe" (Source [+ Schön] row) over the unfolding and labels the order numbers of Schön's row with blue pencil and the order numbers of the source row with graphite pencil.
18. ÖNB Musiksammlung F 21 Berg 28/X, fol. 5r.
19. ÖNB Musiksammlung F 21 Berg 28/X, fol. 4r.
20. Willi Reich, *The Life and Work of Alban Berg*, trans. Cornelius Cardew (London, 1965), p. 64.

Chapter 5

1. Mit meiner jetzigen Arbeit gehts gar nicht gut vorwärts. Es gibt Tage, wo ich mich dieser gewaltigen Aufgabe nicht gewachsen fühle. Wohl auch im Hinblick auf die "Reihen"-Kompositionsart. Ich glaube aber, unlängst eine gute Lösung für das *Problem* gefunden zu haben, mit e i n e r Reihe für so ein mehrstündiges Werk auszukommen. (Abgesehen von diversen Formen, die ich ja schon längst dafür abgeleitet hatte.)
Auf beiliegendem Notenblatt wirst Du sehen, was ich da gefunden habe. Vom mathematischen Standpunkt ist es je [sic] etwas Selbstverständliches. Aber in der musikalischen Praxis der Reihen-Komposition etwas, was vielleicht noch niemand gefunden hat, und das—wie gesagt—auf jede 12 Tonreihe Anwendung finden kann. Handschriftensammlung, Wiener Stadt- und Landesbibliothek I.N. 185.704, fols. 3–4.
2. Douglas Jarman, "*Lulu:* The Sketches," *International Alban Berg Society Newsletter* 6 (June 1978): 6.
3. In the above-mentioned letter to Schoenberg (dated September 1, 1928) Berg reports that he has completed over three hundred measures of *Lulu*.

4. Willi Reich, *The Life and Work of Alban Berg*, trans. Cornelius Cardew (London, 1965), p. 78.

5. Reich, *Alban Berg*, p. 79. Reich's letters to Berg date from October 1928 through 1935, shortly before Berg's death. They are part of the Alban Berg Nachlass in the Musiksammlung of the Österreichische Nationalbibliothek.

6. Reich to Berg, August 30, 1929. ÖNB Musiksammlung F 21 Berg 1234/20.

7. Reich, *Alban Berg*, pp. 79–80. Note that Reich's definition of "complementary row" changes from the specific one appearing in his letters to Berg ("a row whose inversion is identical to its retrograde") to the more general definition that he uses in his Berg biography (*rows* "in which it was possible—on account of their special construction—knowing a few of the notes to deduce the rest"). In the quotation in my text Reich is referring to the *later* definition.

8. Ihre Mitteilungen über Reihentransformation sind fabelhaft interessant und berühen mich ganz besonders tief da sie ganz in die Richtung meiner eigenen Forschungen fallen und sogar meine Kurzschrift welche gleich der Ihren von jeder Transposition unabhängig ist, anticipieren. Scheinbar bestehen hier wirklich höhere Zusammenhange. Dass gerade nur der der [sic] 5. 7. und 11. Ton gehen scheint darin zu liegen das 1 + 11 und 5 + 7 die einzigen reinen Primzahlzerlegungen der Zahl 12 sind, überdies gilt: 5 + 7 + 11 = 23. ÖNB Musiksammlung F 21 Berg 1234/21.

9. Vielen Dank für Ihre liebe Karte, welche mir eine dringend ersehnte Ergänzung zu Ihrer neulich entwickelten Entdeckung der Berg'schen Reihen B5 u. B7 brachte. Nämlich die musikalische Deutung, da das Mathematische doch nur in zweiter Linie für den Musiker in Frage kommt, so interessant es vielleicht auch an sich sein mag. Sehr merkwürdig gestaltet sich auch die Sache wenn man als Originalreihe eine solche von dem von mir aufgezeigten Komplementärtypus nimmt. Dann spielen auch die Umkehrungen allerhand Stückel und der Kreis schliesst sich schon bei den Verwandtschaften ersten Grades. Ich habe einiges auf beiliegendem Notenblatt durchgeführt, es lässt sich aber noch mehr zeigen.

Eine allgemeine Eigenschaft *jeder* B5 und B7 ist folgende: Bei ersterer ist jeder dritte, bei letzterer jeder zweite Ton mit der Originalreihe identisch. ÖNB Musiksammlung F 21 Berg 1234/22.

10. In the opera itself, Geschwitz's row is rarely used in this ordered form. See Douglas Jarman, *The Music of Alban Berg* (Berkeley and Los Angeles, 1979), pp. 121–23.

11. Aus dieser Urreihe (u. jeder 12 Ton Reihe) kann man wenn man *regelmässig* Töne auslässt 2 neue 12 Ton Reihen bilden (u. zw[ar] *nur* 2) u. zw[ar] wenn man 1. jeden 5ten Ton herausgreift: [musical example] und [wenn?] 2. jeden 7ten Ton herausgreift [musical example].

12. Douglas Jarman cites this sketch in connection with Berg's letter to Webern from September 20, 1929, in "*Lulu*: The Sketches," pp. 5–6. Without the aid of Reich's letters he was able to conclude correctly: "The 'attached sheet' of paper, which Berg mentions in his letter, has been lost but it may well have contained some examples and comments very like those which appear in the sketch cited above."

13. Bei jeder anderen Anreihung dieser Art (sei es ob wenn man den 3 4 od[er] 2 3 4 od[er] 5 6 Ton herausgreift) ~~Ton entsteht~~ entstehen nun Reihen mit weniger (bis 2) Tönen, da sie sich früher oder später wiederholen bzw wann man den 8. 9. 10. 11. Ton herausgreift die Krebsform jener 2–6-Tonreihen. Die sind also unbrauchbar. Während die anderen 2 (einzigen) zwar ganz neue Reihen sind, aber doch im engsten u. [missing word] Zusammenhang mit der Urreihe stehen. Dass sie organisch mit jener verwandt sind ergibt sich ~~aus der aus der~~ daraus, dass wenn man (was hier noch nicht geschehen ist)

jeden 11ten Ton herausgreift—(naturlich!) der Krebs der Urreihe ergibt. Womit auch der Kreis geschlossen ist.

14. As I noted in Chapter 2, in *Der Wein* Berg had already used methods of extraction that require shifting to the next note to avoid pitch repetition. In two different row sketches (F 21 Berg 80/II, fols. 5r–6v) Berg forms three- and four-note chords from the source row by extracting every second, third, and fourth note.

15. In the opera, these names are reduced to the titles "The Acrobat" and "The Schoolboy."

16. There is, however, a separate sketch of the derivation of Dr. Schön's row, written (like the two previously cited sketches) on eighteen-staff paper. Since there are only four leaves of eighteen-staff paper among approximately seven hundred leaves of *Lulu* sketches, we can safely assume that these sketches were completed at about the same time.

17. Juliane Brand, Christopher Hailey, and Donald Harris, eds. *The Berg-Schoenberg Correspondence: Selected Letters* (New York, 1987), p. 373.

18. Volker Scherliess has discussed this chart in detail in "Alban Bergs analytische Tafeln zur *Lulu*-Reihe," *Die Musikforschung* 30 (1977): 452–64. Example 33 is based on the transcription that appears in this article.

19. As I noted in Chapter 2, F 21 Berg 28/XXIV includes a draft of the first two scenes of *Lulu* (through ca. m. 520). Near the end of this draft appear several lines from a letter with the date September 30, 1929. I determined from Berg's Tagebuch for 1929 and from his letters to Schoenberg that Berg left his summer residence for Vienna on that day and did not resume composing until the following summer. The Prologue, which contains all the later row forms, was written in 1934. In Chapter 2 I cited an earlier version of the Prologue (dated June 23, 1928); however, it contains none of the later rows.

20. For an excellent summary and discussion of this lengthy and complicated debate, see Jarman, *Music of Alban Berg*, pp. 112–25.

21. George Perle, "The Music of *Lulu*: A New Analysis," *Journal of the American Musicological Society* 12 (1959): 187–88, and "*Lulu*: Thematic Material and Pitch Organization," *Music Review* 26 (1965): 293–96.

22. See the sketch ÖNB Musiksammlung F 21 Berg 28/XX, fol. 5r.

Chapter 6

1. Willi Reich, *The Life and Work of Alban Berg*, trans. Cornelius Cardew (London, 1965), pp. 200–201.

2. The Roman numerals on Berg's draft represent transposition levels. According to Berg's system, the "home key" of a row form is labeled I, the row form a semitone below, II, and so forth. In contrast, I am using Perle's method of labeling, in which row forms beginning on C are labeled P_0, those beginning C sharp, P_1, and so forth.

3. Die Frage, nach welchem Prinzip diese Akkorde verwendet werden und ob sie aus der Grundreihe abgeleitet sind, ist an dieser Stelle von besonderem Interesse, weil sich hier der erste Vorgang der Harmoniebildung als kompositorisches Verfahren darstellt . . . Manfred Reiter, *Die Zwölftontechnik in Alban Bergs Oper "Lulu,"* in *Kölner Beitrage zur Musikforschung*, Band 71 (Regensburg, 1973), p. 16.

4. Bedeutsam ist das Verfahren, in dem die Bild-Harmonien hier eingeführt werden: Im gegensatz zu der von Reich angegebenen Stelle, wo sie als fertige Reihenableitung erscheinen, entstehen sie hier gleichsam erst vor den Ohren des Zuhörers, indem sie sich aus einer VD-Anlage der Grundreihe in den hohen Streichern sukzessive heraus-

kristallisieren, bis sie endlich beim drittenmal (T. 97), mit dem Einsatz der Klarinetten, in ihren Simultangestalt verfestigt sind. Die Ableitung der Bild-Harmonien von der Grundreihe erfolgt also in einem kompositorischen Vorgang. Reiter, *Zwölftontechnik*, p. 67.

5. My observations on closure are based on Christopher Hasty's definition of it in atonal and serial music: "a return to a particular quality" following "a movement away from that quality." See his article "Segmentation and Process in Post-Tonal Music," *Music Theory Spectrum* 3 (1981): 54–73. Notice that in this instance Berg's use of closure is not absolute; the sustained F sharp in the melodic line beginning in m. 89 seems to anticipate, or perhaps form a transition to, the next section (m. 93), where it becomes the upper voice of the Bild Harmonien.

6. Perle discusses this concept in *Serial Composition and Atonality*, 5th ed. (Berkeley and Los Angeles, 1981), p. 77.

7. See the sketch ÖNB Musiksammlung F 21 Berg 28/III, fol. 33r, which I discussed in Chapter 1.

8. The many interruptions that occur in the exposition of the Rondo also necessitate this homogeneity—that is, if the movement is to sound coherent.

9. ÖNB Musiksammlung F 21 Berg 29/I, Act II, scene 1, m. 242 (upper margin).

10. See the sketch ÖNB Musiksammlung F 21 Berg 28/III, fol. 28v.

11. The only citing of this event in the secondary literature is Mark DeVoto's letter to the editor in *In Theory Only* 8, nos. 4–5 (1985): 3.

12. Douglas Jarman, *The Music of Alban Berg* (Berkeley and Los Angeles, 1979), pp. 144–45.

13. Perle, *The Operas of Alban Berg*, vol. 2: "*Lulu*," p. 142.

14. See David Headlam, "The Musical Language of the *Symphonic Pieces* from *Lulu*," Ph.D. Dissertation, University of Michigan, 1985, pp. 233–56.

Concluding Remarks

1. Sherwyn T. Carr, ed., "Future Directions in Sketch Research," in *Beethoven, Performers, and Critics*, ed. Robert Winter and Bruce Carr (Detroit, 1980), p. 144.

2. Carr, "Sketch Research," p. 145.

3. Joseph Kerman, *Contemplating Music* (Cambridge, 1985), p. 94.

4. Anthony Pople, *Berg: Violin Concerto* (Cambridge, 1991), p. 80.

5. George Perle, *The Operas of Alban Berg*, vol. 2: "*Lulu*" (Berkeley and Los Angeles, 1985), p. 294.

Works Cited

Adorno, Theodor W. *Berg: Der Meister des kleinsten Übergangs.* Vienna: Verlag Elisabeth Lafite, 1968.
Berg, Alban. *Letters to His Wife.* Translated by Bernard Grun. New York: St. Martin's Press, 1971.
Berg, Erich Alban, ed. *Alban Berg: Leben und Werk in Daten und Bildern.* Frankfurt: Insel Verlag, 1976.
———. *Der unverbesserliche Romantiker: Alban Berg, 1885–1935.* Vienna: Österreichischer Bundesverlag, 1985.
Brand, Juliane, Christopher Hailey, and Donald Harris, eds. *The Berg-Schoenberg Correspondence: Selected Letters.* New York: Norton, 1987.
Brandenburg, Sieghard, William Drabkin, and Douglas Johnson. "On Beethoven Scholars and Beethoven's Sketches." *Nineteenth-Century Music* 2 (1979): 270–79.
Carner, Mosco. *Alban Berg: The Man and the Work.* London: Duckworth and Co., 1975.
Carr, Bruce, and Robert Winter, eds. *Beethoven, Performers, and Critics.* Detroit: Wayne State University Press, 1980.
Cerha, Friedrich. *Arbeitsbericht zur Herstellung des 3. Akts der Oper "Lulu" von Alban Berg.* Vienna: Universal Edition, 1979.
Eppstein, Hans. "Zu Hugo Wolfs Liedskizzen." *Österreichische Musikzeitschrift* 39 (1984): 645–56.
Ertelt, Thomas F. "'Hereinspaziert...' Ein Früher Entwurf des Prologs zu Alban Bergs *Lulu.*" *Österreichische Musikzeitschrift* 41 (1986): 15–25.

Green, Douglass. "A False Start for *Lulu:* An Early Version of the Prologue." In *Alban Berg: Historical and Analytical Perspectives,* pp. 203–13. Edited by David Gable and Robert Morgan. Oxford: Oxford University Press, 1991.

Hall, Patricia. "The Progress of a Method: Berg's Tone Rows for *Lulu.*" *Musical Quarterly* 71 (1985): 500–519.

———. "Role and Form in Berg's Sketches for *Lulu.*" In *Alban Berg: Historical and Analytical Perspectives,* pp. 235–59. Edited by David Gable and Robert Morgan. Oxford: Oxford University Press, 1991.

———. "The Sketches for *Lulu.*" In *The Berg Companion,* pp. 235–59. Edited by Douglas Jarman. London: Macmillan, 1989.

Hasty, Christopher. "Segmentation and Process in Post-Tonal Music." *Music Theory Spectrum* 3 (1981): 54–73.

Headlam, David. "The Musical Language of the *Symphonic Pieces* from *Lulu.*" Ph.D. Dissertation, University of Michigan, 1985.

Hilmar, Ernst. "Alban Bergs Selbstzeugnisse zu Entstehung und Aufführbarkeit der Oper *Lulu.*" In Alban Berg, *"Lied der Lulu": Faksimile-Ausgabe der Anton V. Webern gewidmeten autographen Partitur,* pp. 12–23. Vienna: Wiener Stadt- und Landesbibliothek, 1985.

———. "Die verschiedenen Entwicklungsstadien in den Kompositionsskizzen." In *50 Jahre Wozzeck von Alban Berg,* pp. 22–26. Edited by Otto Kolleritsch. Graz: Universal Edition, 1978.

Hilmar, Rosemary. *Alban Berg, 1885–1935: Katalog zur Ausstellung der Österreichischen Nationalbibliothek.* Vienna: Universal Edition, 1985.

———. *Katalog der Musikhandschriften, Schriften und Studien Alban Bergs im Fond Alban Berg und der weiteren handschriftlichen Quellen im Besitz der Österreichischen Nationalbibliothek.* Alban Berg Studien, Band I. Vienna: Universal Edition, 1980.

Hyde, Martha. "The Format and Function of Schoenberg's Twelve-Tone Sketches." *Journal of the American Musicological Society* 36 (1983): 453–80.

Jancik, Hans, ed. *Hugo Wolf, Sämtliche Werke,* Band 19, no. 1: *Fragmente und Skizzen.* Vienna: Musikwissenschaftlicher Verlag, 1992.

Jarman, Douglas. "Alban Berg, Wilhelm Fliess, and the Secret Programme of the Violin Concerto." *International Alban Berg Society Newsletter* 12 (Fall/Winter 1982): 5–11.

———. "*Lulu:* The Sketches." *International Alban Berg Society Newsletter* 6 (June 1978): 4–8.

———. *The Music of Alban Berg.* Berkeley and Los Angeles: University of California Press, 1979.

Johnson, Douglas. "Beethoven Scholars and Beethoven's Sketches." *Nineteenth-Century Music* 2 (1978): 3–17.

Kerman, Joseph. *Contemplating Music.* Cambridge: Harvard University Press, 1985.

Kraus, Karl. "Die Büchse der Pandora." In *Literatur und Lüge*, pp. 5–15. Munich: Kösel-Verlag, 1958.

Lockwood, Lewis. "The Autograph of the First Movement of Beethoven's Sonata for Violoncello and Pianoforte, Opus 69." In *The Music Forum*, vol. 2, pp. 1–109. Edited by William Mitchell and Felix Salzer. New York: Columbia University Press, 1970.

Mahler, Alma. *Mein Leben*. Berlin: S. Fischer Verlag, 1960.

Perle, George. "The Film Interlude of *Lulu*." *International Alban Berg Society Newsletter* 11 (Spring 1982): 3–8.

———. "*Lulu*: Thematic Material and Pitch Organization." *Music Review* 26 (November 1965): 269–302.

———. "The Music of *Lulu*: A New Analysis." *Journal of the American Musicological Society* 12 (1959): 185–200.

———. *The Operas of Alban Berg*, vol. 2: "*Lulu*." Berkeley and Los Angeles: University of California Press, 1985.

———. *Serial Composition and Atonality*. 5th edition. Berkeley and Los Angeles: University of California Press, 1981.

Pople, Anthony. *Berg: Violin Concerto*. Cambridge: Cambridge University Press, 1991.

Redlich, Hans F. *Alban Berg: The Man and His Music*. New York: Abelard-Schuman, 1957.

———. *Alban Berg: Versuch einer Würdigung*. Vienna: Universal Edition, 1957.

Reich, Willi. "Alban Berg's *Lulu*." *Musical Quarterly* 22 (1936): 383–401.

———. "An der Seite von Alban Berg." *Melos* 27 (1960): 36–42.

———. *The Life and Work of Alban Berg*. Translated by Cornelius Cardew. London: Thames and Hudson, 1965.

Reiter, Manfred. *Die Zwölftontechnik in Alban Bergs Oper "Lulu."* In *Kölner Beitrage zur Musikforschung*, Band 71. Edited by Heinrich Huschen. Regensburg: Gustav Bosse Verlag, 1973.

Schachter, Carl. "Beethoven's Sketches for the First Movement of Op. 14, No. 1: A Study in Design." *Journal of Music Theory* 26, no. 1 (1982): 1–21.

Scherliess, Volker. "Alban Bergs analytische Tafeln zur *Lulu*-Reihe." *Die Musikforschung* 30 (1977): 452–64.

Schweizer, Klaus. *Die Sonatensatzform im Schaffen Alban Bergs*. Stuttgart: Musikwissenschaftliche Verlags-Gesellschaft, 1970.

Wedekind, Frank. *Erdgeist / Die Büchse der Pandora. Tragödien*. Edited by Peter Unger and Harmut Vinçon. Munich: Wilhelm Goldmann Verlag, 1980.

Youens, Susan. "The Song Sketches of Hugo Wolf." *Current Musicology* 44 (1990): 5–37.

Index

"Aachen sketch," 43, 46 fig.18
Act I, coda of: fate rhythm of, 100; reordering of rows in, 153; repeated sketches of, 100, 101 fig.24, 102 ex.26A–C, 103; unfolding for, 103, 104 ex.27, 171n17
Act I, scene 1, Duet of: complicated row manipulations in, 141–43; compositional sketches of, 140 fig.42, 141; musical passage of, 138 ex.39; repeated textual idea of, 139
Act I, scene 1, opening passage of: compositional sketches of, 35, 36 fig.12; triadic configurations of, 132–34 ex.35, 135–37, 136 exx.37,38; twelve-tone organization of, 130–31 fig.41, 135, 173n2; use of closure in, 137, 174n5
Act I, scene 2, Monorhythmica of: form sketch of, 21, 23 fig.6
Act I, scene 2, Sonata of: constructed in two halves, 91–92; form sketches of, 21, 22 fig.5, 92, 93 fig.32, 94 ex.22A,B; theme/character pairings of, 92, 95, 143–44; unfolding of main theme of, 95–97, 98 fig.33a,b, 99. *See also* Act I, coda of
Act II, Rondo of: association of different row forms in, 149, 151, 153; homogeneous themes of, 143–44, 145 ex.43, 174n8; palindromic structure of, 145–46; reordering of Alwa's row in, 152 ex.50, 153–54; sketch of form and dramatic symbolism for, 146, 147 fig.43; use/exclusion of tonality in, 145
Act II, scene 1: row derivation controversy of, 89–90; Schön's unfolding in, 99–100, 103, 105, 106–7 ex.28

Act III, scene 2: form sketch of, 20 fig.4, 21
Address stamps, 166n7, 167n23
Adorno, Theodor: Berg's correspondence with, 30–31, 167n21; on Berg's twelve-tone technique, 16
"Alban Berg, Wilhelm Fliess, and the Secret Programme of the *Violin Concerto*" (Jarman), 71
Alban Berg Nachlass, 15, 165n1
Alwa (*Lulu*): in "déjà vu" pairing, 80; themes' depiction of, 143–44, 145–46, 149; vocal delivery of, 144
Alwa's row: compositional reordering of, 148 fig.44, 150 ex.47, 151, 152 exx.49,50, 153–54; derivation of, 18 ex.8, 111, 117; derivation of subsidiary rows from, 148 fig.44, 149, 150 exx.45,46, 151; grafted passages of, 123; twelve transpositions of, 17, 18 fig.2
Animal Trainer, the (*Lulu*), 76–77
Ast, Max, 28
Autograph sources: Berg's Tagebuch, 39, 40, 52, 173n19; gold-edged notebook, 38, 62, 63, 169nn4,7; location and types of, 15–16, 165n1; for 1927, 31, 32 fig.9, 166n13; for 1928, 33, 34 fig.10, 35, 36 fig.12, 37 fig.13, 167n21, 167nn23–26; for 1929, 38–40, 41 fig.14, 167–68n32; for 1930, 43, 44 fig.16, 45 fig.17, 46 fig.18, 47; for 1931, 47, 48 fig.19, 49, 50 fig.20, 51 fig.21, 52, 53 fig.22; for 1932, 52, 168n48; for 1933–35, 55–56, 57 fig.23, 58 fig.24, 59; problematic dating of, 28, 40–41, 166nn1,2; as source of *Lulu* scholarship, 3–4; tech-

niques for dating, 29–30, 166nn4–7. *See also* Berg's correspondence; Berg's sketches

Banker, the (*Lulu*), 76, 170nn23,25
Beethoven, Ludwig van, 4, 13. *See also* Sonata Opus 14, no. 1
Berg, Alban: compositional process of, 25, 27, 161, 165nn12,13, 166n14; illness and death of, 59; musical handwriting of, 14; numerology interest of, 33, 40; Reich's biography of, 2; Schoenberg's twelve-tone system *vs.*, 3; serial technique of, 12; use of jazz forms by, 39, 167n31; "Why Is Schoenberg's Music So Difficult to Understand?," 128. *See also* Berg's correspondence; Berg's sketches
Berg, Helene, 3, 56
Bergian row B_5: derivation of, 111, 112 fig.35, 113, 114 fig.36, 115, 116 fig.37, 172n12
Bergian row B_7: derivation of, 111, 112 fig.35, 113, 114 fig.36, 115, 116 fig.37, 172n12
Berg's correspondence: as chronological source, 15–16, 29, 33, 38, 39–40, 45 fig.17, 52, 53 fig.22, 55–56, 119, 123, 166n4, 167n21, 167nn25,26, 167–68n32, 172n5, 173n19; on form of *Lulu*, 61; incorrect dating of, 28; on material deprivation, 55; on plans for second opera, 30–31; on progress of *Lulu*, 33, 43, 47, 49, 52, 55, 56, 167n21, 168n48, 171n3; with Reich on complementary rows, 110–11, 172n7; on row derivation discovery, 38–39, 109, 117, 119; on symmetry of center scenes, 75–76; on *Der Wein* commission, 38
Berg's sketches: analytical potential of, 4, 12–13; conservative transcription of, 14; featuring graphic notation, 56, 58 fig.24, 59, 97, 98 fig.33a; lack of immediate revision in, 25, 26, 35; letters drafted on, 29, 166n4; of multiple roles, 63, 65 ex.11, 65 fig.26, 66–67, 68 ex.12A,B, 68 fig.27; organic analysis of, 162; problematic chronology of, 15, 28, 33, 165n3, 166nn1,2; in "Sommer 1930, erledigt" folder, 40–41, 42 fig.15, 43; as source of *Lulu* scholarship, 3–4; text/musical theme pairings in, 80–81, 82 fig.31, 84 ex.18A,B, 86 ex.19A, 87 ex.19B, 92, 95, 139; as variants on Hyde's categories, 17, 18 fig.2, 19 fig.3, 21, 24–25, 26 fig.8. *See also* Compositional sketches; Concept sketches; Form sketches; Row charts; Row sketches
Bild Harmonien, 139 ex.40; derivation of, 135–36; row forms assigned to, 119, 121–22 ex.33d, 123
Bob the Groom (*Lulu*), 77
"Bordell ist Ehe" (brothel is marriage) theme, 71, 73, 75–76
Brown, Alyson, 169n10
Büchner, Georg, 30
Die Büchse der Pandora (Wedekind): as autograph source, 15, 38, 165n13; Berg's opera plans and, 30; joining of *Erdgeist* to, 61, 63; Kraus's lecture on, 75, 165n3, 170n30

Carner, Mosco, 31, 89
Cerha, Friedrich, 73, 162
Chronology of sketches: importance and usefulness of, 161–62; as problematic, 28, 40–41, 166nn1,2; techniques for determining, 29–30, 166nn4–7. *See also* Autograph sources
Circus theme, 76–77
Clients. *See* Victim/client doublings
Coda of Act I. *See* Act I, coda of
Complementary series: derivation of B_5 and B_7 from, 111, 112 fig.35, 113 ex.30; Reich's definition of, 110, 172n7
Compositional sketches: of Act I, scene 1, 35, 36 fig.12; of conclusion of Act I, 47, 48 fig.19; of Duet of Act I, scene 1, 140 fig.42, 141; Hyde's category of, 16–17; as realization of musical passage, 17, 21; shorthand, 17, 19 fig.3; thematic, 17, 18 fig.2; of Variations, 155, 157 fig.46
Concept sketches: date manipulation on, 40, 41 fig.14; described, 21, 24; ideas for orchestration in, 27; of the Prologue, 33, 35 fig.11

Dramatic symbolism: expressed through unfoldings, 91, 105, 108; linking triple roles, 71, 72 fig.29, 73, 74 fig.30, 75–77, 170nn23,25; in Lulu and Schigolch's duets, 80–81, 82 fig.31, 83 ex.17A,B, 84 ex.18A, 85 ex.18B, 86 ex.19A, 87 ex.19B; of Rondo of Act II, 146; sketch of, 24–25, 26 fig.8; through character's reworking, 80, 170n28. *See also* Multiple roles

Dresser, the (*Lulu*), 77

Duet of Act I, scene 1. *See* Act I, scene 1, Duet of

English Waltz, 73
Eppstein, Hans, 165n20
Erdgeist fourths, 149
Erdgeist (Wedekind): as autograph source, 15, 38, 165n13; Berg's opera plans and, 30; joining of *Büchse der Pandora* to, 61, 63; omitted scenes of, 66
Extended tonality: sketch analysis based on, 7, 9, 11

"The Format and Function of Schoenberg's Twelve-Tone Sketches" (Hyde), 165n7
Form sketches: for Act III, scene 2, 20 fig.4, 21; Hyde's category of, 17; of *Lulu*'s large-scale form, 62–63, 64 ex.10, 64 fig.25; meter component of, 21, 22 fig.5, 23 fig.6; for rejected sonata exposition, 35, 37 fig.13; for Rondo of Act II, 143–44, 146, 147 fig. 43; for Sonata of Act I, 92, 93 fig.32; symmetry feature of, 21

Geschwitz's row, 49, 50 fig.20, 51 fig.21; derivation of, 111, 117
"Der Glücksritter" (Wolf): sketch analysis of, 7, 8 ex.4, 9, 10 exx.5,6, 10 fig.1, 11, 164n18
Gold-edged notebook: ideas on symbolism and form in, 62–63; problematic dating of, 38, 63, 169n4, 169n7
Goll, Dr. (*Lulu*): in multiple roles, 63, 65 fig.26, 66, 67, 70, 169n2
Gropius, Manon, 59

Handwriting evidence, 166n7
Hasty, Christopher, 174n5

Hauptmann, Gerhart, 30, 31
Hilmar, Rosemary, 15, 28, 40, 41, 47, 59
Hilti, Dr. (*Lulu*), 66
Hugenberg, the Schoolboy (*Lulu*), 77, 80, 117
Hunidei, Herr (*Lulu*): in multiple roles, 66, 67, 70
Hyde, Martha, 16, 165n7

Ideen sketches. *See* Concept sketches

Jack the Ripper (*Lulu*): in multiple roles, 66, 67, 70
Jarman, Douglas: analytical sketch study by, 3, 4; on Berg's borrowed tunes, 71; on Berg's compositional discovery, 109; on Reich's one-row hypothesis, 97; on row sketch of B_5 and B_7, 172n12; on triple role, 170n25; on Variations, 155
Jazz, 39, 167n31
"Das Jazzbuch," 39, 167n31
Johnson, Douglas, 4, 5

Kerman, Joseph, 162
Kleiber, Erich, 55
Kraus, Karl, 73, 75, 81, 170n30
Kungu Poti (*Lulu*), 66, 67

"Lautenlied" (Wedekind), 154. *See also* Variations
Lockwood, Lewis, 13
Lohengrin wedding march, 71, 73, 170n15
Loos, Adolf, 43, 44 fig.16
Lulu (Berg): correspondence on progress of, 33, 43, 47, 49, 52, 55, 56, 167n21, 168n48, 171n3; earliest dated source for, 31, 32 fig.9, 33, 166n13; location/types of autograph sources for, 15–16, 165n1; nonconsecutive composition of, 28, 33, 38, 39–40, 166n2, 167–68n32; one-row controversy of, 89–90, 96–97, 123, 125, 135; orchestration of, 27, 59, 162, 166n14; palindromic structure of, 61–62, 63, 75–76, 81; Perle's study of, 3–4, 164n9; Reich's study of, 2; sketch analysis of, 4, 12–13; weakness of secondary literature on, 129

Lulu (*Lulu*): in duets with Schigolch, 80–81, 82 fig.31, 83 ex.17A,B, 84 ex.18A, 85 ex.18B, 86 ex.19A, 87 ex.19B; scale form assigned to, 119, 121–22 ex.33e
Lyric Suite (Berg), 135

Mahler, Anna, 43, 45 fig.17, 168n38
Manservant, the (*Lulu*): Rodrigo's musical association with, 76, 78–79 ex.16A,B, 170n22; in triple role, 71, 72 fig.29
Manservant's row, 108
Marquis, the (*Lulu*): in triple role, 71, 72 fig.29, 73, 74 fig.30, 75
Marriage theme. *See* "Bordell ist Ehe" theme
Meter: as feature of form sketches, 21, 22 fig.5, 23 fig.6; musical themes paired with, 95, 158, 159 fig.47, 160
Monorhythmica of Act I, scene 2. *See* Act I, scene 2, Monorhythmica of
Multiple roles: based on opera's large-scale symmetry, 21, 67, 69 ex.13A,B, 69 fig.28, 70, 75–76, 81; Berg's correspondence on, 61; discussed in gold-edged notebook, 38, 62–63; as dramatic associations, 66–67, 68 ex.12A,B, 68 fig.27; as predetermined pairings, 63, 65 ex.11, 65 fig.26, 66; primary effects and purpose of, 61–62; reflected in musical themes, 70–71, 72 fig.29, 73, 74 fig.30; summary of, 88 ex.20. *See also* Dramatic symbolism
Musical themes: as facets of personality, 143–44, 145 ex.43, 146, 174n8; pairing of meter with, 95, 158, 159 fig.47, 160; pairing of text themes with, 80–81, 82 fig.31, 84 ex.18A,B, 86 ex.19A, 87 ex.19B, 92, 95, 139; reflection of multiple roles in, 70–71, 72 fig.29, 73, 74 fig.30; sketches' discernment of, 27, 165n12
"The Music of *Lulu*: A New Analysis" (Perle), 3
Musiksammlung of the Österreichische Nationalbibliothek, 3, 15

One-row controversy, 89–90, 96–97, 123, 125, 135
Orchestration stage, 27, 59, 166n14

Österreichische Nationalbibliothek, 3, 4, 15, 165n3

Painter, the (*Lulu*). *See* Schwarz, the Painter
Pandora's Box. *See Die Büchse der Pandora*
Paper types: as chronological evidence, 29, 31, 33, 35, 47, 54, 166n5, 167n23, 173n16
Particell (Berg): analysis of twelve-tone variation in, 155, 156 fig.45; as autograph source, 15, 144, 146, 165n4; new compositional method in, 119, 123, 124 fig.40, 126 ex.34A, 127 ex.34B; Perle's sketch research on, 3–4
Perle, George: on Berg's use of twelve-tone system, 3, 155; on Cerha's orchestration of Act III, 162; on coda of the Sonata, 100; on multiple roles, 67, 70, 76–77, 169n10, 170n25; on one-row hypothesis, 90, 96–97, 125; research on autograph sources by, 3–4, 164n9
Police Commissioner, the (*Lulu*), 76, 170nn23,25
Pople, Anthony, 162
Prince, the (*Lulu*): in triple role, 71, 72 fig.29, 73, 75
Prologue: abandoned 1928 sketch of, 33, 34 fig.10; compositional sketches of, 56, 57 fig.23; concept sketch of, 33, 35 fig.11; graphic notation in sketch of, 56, 58 fig.24, 59; later row forms in, 173n19

Redlich, Hans, 100
Reich, Willi: on complementary series, 110, 111, 172n7; on derivation of subsidiary rows, 3, 164n9; *Lulu* program notes of, 2, 59; one-row hypothesis of, 89–90; on victim/client doublings, 73, 75
Reiter, Manfred, 135–36
"Revenge of the world of men" theme, 67, 70, 73, 75, 81, 170n30
Rodrigo, the Acrobat (*Lulu*): Manservant's musical association with, 76, 78–79 ex.16A,B, 170n22; in multiple roles, 63, 65 fig.6, 66, 67, 76–77
Rondo of Act II. *See* Act II, Rondo of
Row charts: for Countess Geschwitz, 49, 50 fig.20, 51 fig.21; Hilmar's dating

of, 28; Hyde's category of, 16; as
  Lulu's earliest dated source, 31, 32
  fig.9, 33, 166n13; of 1927 row derivation methods, 119, 120 fig.39; of
  twelve transpositions of Alwa's row,
  17, 18 fig.2, 148 fig.44
Row derivation: of B_5 and B_7, 111, 112
  fig.35, 113, 114 fig.36, 115, 116 fig.37,
  172n12; Berg's innovation in, 38–39,
  54, 109–11, 117, 119, 123; juxtaposed
  methods of, 123, 124 fig.24, 126
  ex.34A, 127 ex.34B; 1927 methods
  of, 119, 120 fig.39, 121–22 ex.33, 123;
  one-row controversy of, 89–90,
  96–97, 123, 125, 135; and pitch duplication, 115, 117, 151, 173n14; Reich's
  complementary series and, 110, 111,
  172n7; of Schön's row, 90, 95–96, 97,
  99–100, 101 fig.34, 102 ex.26A–C,
  103, 117, 119 ex.32, 171n16, 173n16;
  of subsidiary rows from source row,
  3, 38–39, 164n9; of triads of opening
  passage, 132–34 ex.35, 135–37, 136
  exx.37,38; *Der Wein's* sketches and,
  39, 41, 42 fig.15. *See also* Unfoldings
Row forms: assigned to characters, 40, 117,
  118 fig.38; Berg's association of different, 3, 54, 148 fig.44, 149, 150
  exx.45–47, 151, 152 ex.49, 153; in
  opening passage of Act I, scene I,
  130–31 fig.41, 131, 135, 136 ex.36,
  173n2
Row sketches: Berg's experimentation
  with, 17, 18 fig.2, 25; connection of
  earlier and later styles in, 150
  exx.45,46, 151; of derivation of B_5
  and B_7, 112 fig.35, 114 fig.36, 115,
  116 fig.37; Hyde's category of, 16

Schachter, Carl: sketch analysis of
  Beethoven by, 5–7, 11
"Scherge" (hangman's assistant) theme, 76
Schiedrowitz, Leo, 56
Schigolch (*Lulu*): in duets with Lulu,
  80–81, 82 fig.31, 83 ex.17A,B, 84
  ex.18A, 85 ex.18B, 86 ex.19A, 87
  ex.19B; in victim/client pairings, 63,
  65 fig.26
Schigolch's row, 119, 121–22 ex.33h, 150
  ex.46, 151
Schloss, Julius: and Geschwitz's row chart,
  49, 50 fig.20, 51 fig.21

Schoenberg, Arnold: correspondence on
  row derivation with, 28, 109, 117,
  119; *Lulu* progress reports to, 33, 43,
  47, 49, 52, 53 fig.22, 167n21, 168n48,
  171n3; twelve-tone system of, 3
Schoenberg, Dorothese Nuria, 52
Schön, Dr. (*Lulu*): in multiple roles, 63, 65
  fig.6, 66, 67, 70, 169n2; represented in
  Sonata of Act I, 91–92. *See also*
  Unfoldings
Schön's row: cyclic derivation of, 90, 90
  ex.21, 95–96, 97, 99–100, 101 fig.34,
  102 ex.26A–C, 103, 117, 119 ex.32,
  171n16, 173n16; grafted passages of,
  123, 127 ex.34B; one-row hypothesis
  and, 89–90; retrograde evolution of,
  89, 105
Schoolboy, the (*Lulu*). *See* Hugenberg, the
  Schoolboy
"Der Schreckenberger" (Wolf), 9, 164n18
Schwarz, the Painter (*Lulu*): in multiple
  role, 63, 65 fig.6, 66, 67, 169nn2,10
Schweizer, Klaus, 91, 95, 99–100
Serial technique, 12
Shorthand sketches: described, 17, 19 fig.3
Sketch analysis: of highly defined systems,
  11–12; of tonal systems, 4–7; of transitional compositional systems, 7, 9, 11
Sketchbooks: as autograph source, 33, 35,
  47, 167n23
Sketches of dramatic symbolism:
  described, 24–25, 26 fig.8. *See also*
  Dramatic symbolism
Sketching technique: as chronological evidence, 29, 167n23
Slavery theme. *See* "Bordell ist Ehe" theme
"Sommer 1930, erledigt" (folder): as autograph source, 40–41, 42 fig.15, 43
Sonata of Act I, scene 2. *See* Act I, scene 2,
  Sonata of
Sonata Opus 14, no. 1 (Beethoven): sketch
  analysis of, 5–6
Source row: derivation of subsidiary rows
  from, 3, 38–39, 164n9; one-row
  hypothesis and, 89–90. *See also* Row
  derivation
Subsidiary rows: derived from source row,
  3, 38–39, 89–90, 164n9. *See also* Row
  derivation

Theater Director, the (*Lulu*), 76, 170nn23,25
Thematic sketches: described, 17, 18 fig.2

Tonality: sketch analysis based on, 4–7
Triple roles: dramatic symbolism linking, 71, 72 fig.29, 73, 74 fig.30, 75–77, 170nn23,25; split into symmetrical pairs, 77, 80
Twelve-tone row technique: of Berg vs. Schoenberg, 3; developed in Variations, 16, 154–55, 156 fig.45, 157 fig.46, 158, 159 fig.47, 160; second period shift in, 54; sketches' clarification of, 12–13. *See also* Row derivation; Row forms
Twelve-tone sketches: Berg's variants of, 17, 18 fig.2, 19 fig.3, 21, 24–25, 26 fig.8; Hyde's categories of, 16–17, 18 fig.2, 19 fig.3, 20 fig.4. *See also* Compositional sketches; Concept sketches; Form sketches; Row charts; Row sketches

Und Pippa Tanzt! (Hauptmann), 30, 31
Unfoldings: for coda of Act I, scene 1, 103, 104 ex.27, 171n17; expressive of dramatic symbolism, 91, 105, 108; of main theme of Sonata of Act I, scene 2, 95–97, 99; and one-row controversy, 90–91, 96–97; in Schön's death scene, 99–100, 103, 105, 106–7 ex.28. *See also* Row derivation

Variations: metric parameters of, 158, 159 fig.47, 160; use of twelve-tone composition in, 16, 154–55, 156 fig.45, 157 fig.46
Vergeltung (revenge) theme. *See* "Revenge of the world of men" theme
Victim/client doublings: in dramatic associations, 67, 68 ex.12A,B, 68 fig.27, 70; inspired by Kraus, 73, 75; in predetermined pairings, 63, 65 ex.11, 65 fig.26, 66; symmetry of, 61. *See also* Multiple roles
Violin Concerto (Berg), 59, 125, 162

Webern, Anton: correspondence on row derivation with, 38–39, 109, 119; *Lulu* progress reports to, 47, 49, 55, 56, 165n4, 166n14
Wedekind, Frank, 30, 73. *See also Die Büchse der Pandora*; *Erdgeist*
Weill, Kurt, 73
Der Wein (Berg), 38–39, 40–41, 42 fig.15, 135
"Why Is Schoenberg's Music So Difficult to Understand?" (Berg), 128
Wolf, Hugo, 7; compositional process of, 9, 165n20. *See also* "Der Glücksritter"
Woyzeck (Büchner), 30
Wozzeck (Berg), 30, 43
Writing implements: as chronological evidence, 29, 31, 33, 166n6, 167nn23,24

Zsolnay, Paul, 43

Designer: Steve Renick
Compositor: Impressions Book and Journal Services, Inc.
Text: 11/13.5 Bembo
Display: Bembo

www.ingramcontent.com/pod-product-compliance
Lightning Source LLC
Chambersburg PA
CBHW021708230426
43668CB00008B/763